HEALTH REPORTS:
DISEASES AND DISORDERS

STDs

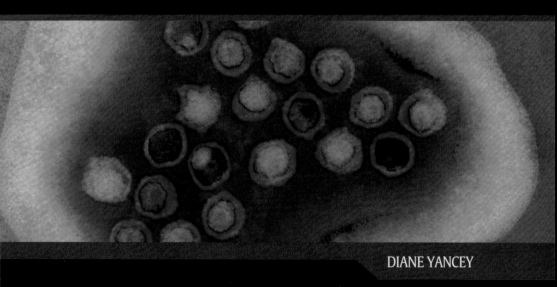

DIANE YANCEY

TF
CB TWENTY-FIRST CENTURY BOOKS
MINNEAPOLIS

Twenty-First Century Books
A division of Lerner Publishing Group, Inc.
241 First Avenue North
Minneapolis, MN 55401 U.S.A.

Website address: www.lernerbooks.com

Library of Congress Cataloging-in-Publication Data

Yancey, Diane.
    STDs / by Diane Yancey.
        p. cm. — (USA Today health reports: Diseases and disorders)
    Includes bibliographical references and index.
    ISBN 978-0-7613-5456-7 (lib. bdg. : alk. paper)
    1. Sexually transmitted diseases—Juvenile literature. I. Title. II. Series.
    RC200.25.Y35 2012
    616.95'1—dc22   2010036514

Manufactured in the United States of America
1 – MG – 7/15/11

CONTENTS

USA TODAY
HEALTH REPORTS:
DISEASES AND DISORDERS

UP CLOSE AND PERSONAL

For most teenagers, relationships are a top priority. The world would seem lonely and meaningless without friends to talk to, rely on, and love. But relationships, especially sexual relationships, can be complicated. The emotions and feelings that arise while falling in and out of love can sometimes be bewildering and difficult to sort out.

Sexual feelings are extremely strong when two people fall in love. Many couples, however, have not thought about their own sexual values and limits before beginning a relationship. Caught up in their feelings for one another, they don't always think about the outcomes of their actions. In the rush to experience sexual intimacy, they may give little thought to whether they are risking pregnancy, illness, or even death. When they do stop to consider these risks, it is sometimes too late.

The experiences of the teens in this book illustrate what happens when inadequate planning, poor judgment, or the thoughtlessness of others lead to sexual health problems. These young people are coping with sexually transmitted diseases (STDs)—bacterial or viral infections that can be passed from person to person during intimate sexual contact. All the teens in this book have learned that STDs can affect anyone. Most are now planning to practice safe sex to better protect their health.

NAKEESHA AND SERGIO

Nakeesha and Sergio are both seventeen years old. They plan to marry, and they already have a one-year-old daughter, Alicia. Three months ago, Nakeesha discovered that she was pregnant again.

Recently, Nakeesha woke up with a dull pain in her lower abdomen. The pain didn't go away. She felt, at times, as if she might have a fever. After a few days, she went to a doctor, who diagnosed her pain as pelvic inflammatory disease (PID), an infection often caused by an STD. A test revealed that Nakeesha also had chlamydia, a sexually transmitted disease that is common among teens.

Now Nakeesha wonders what effect her STD will have on her unborn baby's health and well-being. She doesn't think she can talk to Sergio about her STD, but the doctor says that Sergio, too, must get medical treatment. If he doesn't, Nakeesha will probably get the STD again.

CELESTE

Sixteen-year-old Celeste is president of her sophomore class in high school. At the end of Celeste's freshman year, she went to a party at a friend's house. Somebody brought alcohol to the party along with chips and videos. Somehow things got out of hand, and Celeste ended up having sex in a bedroom upstairs with a guy she barely knew.

Later that summer, while getting a sports physical, Celeste asked her doctor about some embarrassing symptoms she was having. After testing, the doctor told Celeste that she had gonorrhea, a sexually transmitted disease. Celeste was shocked. She had heard of gonorrhea, but she had always believed that only prostitutes and promiscuous girls could catch it. Now she had to revise her opinions. She realized that she didn't know very much about sexually transmitted diseases after all.

LEAH AND DANIEL

Leah and Daniel met each other at the end of their sophomore year in high school. They have dated for three months and talk about getting married and having sex as soon as they graduate. For Daniel, however,

two years seems like a long time to wait to have sex. Leah is willing to be patient but wants to please Daniel more than anything else.

Leah decided to share her mixed feelings with her older sister, Susan. Susan suggested that Leah visit a doctor or health clinic to get information on birth control before going "all the way." At the clinic, a nurse-counselor gave Leah literature and condoms (close-fitting latex coverings worn over the penis during sexual intercourse to prevent pregnancy and the spread of STDs). She suggested that both Leah and Daniel be tested for STDs before engaging in sexual behavior. Leah thinks it's a good suggestion, but Daniel thinks she's making a big to-do about nothing.

NATHAN

Nathan is a bisexual teen who lives on the streets of Seattle, Washington. He ran away from home two years ago as a result of ongoing conflict with his parents. Like many of his street friends, Nathan turned to prostitution to live and to support his drug use.

One night last year, Nathan was beaten up by one of his customers and ended up in the hospital. There, a doctor broke the news that Nathan tested positive for human immunodeficiency virus (HIV), the virus that causes acquired immunodeficiency syndrome (AIDS). Nathan was shocked, but he pretended the news didn't bother him. He accepted the medications the doctor gave him and took them regularly for a while. Only after two of Nathan's friends died of drug overdoses in the same week did he begin to reevaluate his behavior and the direction and purpose of his life.

MIGUEL AND LARISSA

Larissa is Miguel's dream girl—tall, beautiful, and intelligent. More important, she seems to love Miguel very much. Miguel has been sexually intimate with his last two girlfriends, and he's hoping that Larissa will want to have sex with him soon. He's a little nervous, however. Some alarming growths on his penis have recently been diagnosed as genital warts, an STD caused by a virus. The doctor he went to told him that the warts were incurable and highly infectious and that Miguel should always wear a condom during sex. Even then, there would be no guarantee that he would not infect his partner.

Miguel knows he would feel bad if he gave Larissa genital warts. Still, he doesn't know if he'll do anything about the situation. Embarrassed and worried, Miguel hopes that his genital warts are not as big a deal as the doctor says they are.

Knowledge can make a real difference in how teens behave when it comes to sex, sexual orientation, and pregnancy. This means understanding the prevalence of STDs, their symptoms, how they're passed on, and how they can be treated. Learning about STDs is an important first step in protecting the sexual health of millions of American teens like those profiled in this book.

In the following chapters, you will have the opportunity to learn about the main STDs that affect young people. This book will make clear how to avoid catching these diseases and how to live with and manage STDs for which there are no cures. First, however, it is important to be familiar with the behavior and the attitudes that put teens at risk for catching STDs.

CHAPTER ONE

WHY WORRY?

D o you know that you could have an STD and not know it? Do you know that in the United States, teens are at the highest risk among all age groups for getting an STD? Do you know that you can catch an STD without "going all the way"? Do you know that women are more at risk than men for catching some STDs?

Sexually transmitted diseases were once known as venereal diseases (VDs), named after Venus, the Roman goddess of love. They have infected humankind for centuries. The ancient Greek physician Galen gave gonorrhea its name in the second century A.D. The disease was also well known to the ancient Chinese and Egyptians. Syphilis was the scourge of Europe from the sixteenth through the nineteenth centuries, killing hundreds of thousands of people. Although recognized as physical afflictions, neither gonorrhea nor syphilis was well understood. For a time, they were even believed to be one disease, probably because people were often infected with both at the same time.

The discovery of antibiotics in the 1930s and 1940s provided a cure for both gonorrhea and syphilis. Still, these diseases continue to infect millions of people around the world.

TEENS AT HIGHER RISK

Our ancestors knew about only two major STDs—syphilis and gonorrhea. By the twenty-first century, medical professionals have identified more than twenty diseases that can be transmitted sexually. Some, such as chancroid and Donovanosis, are rare in the United States. Others, such as trichomoniasis (an infection that causes genital discharge, burning, and itching), are common but, though uncomfortable, are not considered dangerous. Fewer than half of the known STDs pose serious threats to public health in the United States. Still, sexually transmitted diseases infect humans in record numbers in the twenty-first century, and some—such as HIV/AIDS—can be deadly. The United States leads the world in the rate of STDs, with at least nineteen million new cases annually through 2010.

Teens, young adults and STDs

People ages 15 to 24 accounted for one-quarter of the sexually active population in 2000, but they suffered for nearly half of the cases of eight sexually transmitted diseases. Number of cases:

Ages 15 to 24	Total
9.1 million	18.9 million

Source: *Perspectives on Sexual and Reproductive Health*   By Karl Gelles, USA TODAY, 2004

Why should teens worry about those figures? The answer is simple: teenagers have the highest rate of STD infection of any age group in the United States. One out of four teenagers is infected each year, and it is estimated that more than nine million new cases involve people under the age of twenty-five. Young people are becoming sexually active at younger and younger ages. STD infections are threatening their ability to have children, increasing their risk of cancer and other diseases and, in some cases, threatening their lives. Life-threatening STDs like HIV/AIDS are a growing threat to teens, but many mistakenly believe that HIV/ AIDS is now curable. Better education is crucial to preventing such misconceptions.

WHY HAVEN'T STDs DISAPPEARED?

In the age of antibiotics and modern medicine, why do STDs continue to pose a threat to human health? There are a variety of reasons, which include:

LACK OF INFORMATION

Educating people about STDs has always been difficult. Many Americans believe that anything relating to sex is a private topic and that talking about it is in poor taste. Some have never been taught about sex and don't want to reveal their ignorance. Some adults don't talk to their children about sexual matters because they believe that young people who are informed are more likely to be sexually active.

Sex education classes in schools usually offer comprehensive information about STDs, but these classes are sometimes boring or preachy. Students are often turned off by the way material is presented and tune it out. Some teens do not attend class regularly or drop out of school and miss the message altogether. Media

Students often take sex education classes in school but can find them boring. Or they may be turned off by the way the subject is discussed.

messages about the risks of STDs are more attention-getting. These, however, can only give general advice rather than detailed, accurate information about preventing STDs or getting treatment if you have one.

EMBARRASSMENT

Many people don't talk about STDs with their sexual partners because they are embarrassed. It is hard to bring up a discussion of sex with someone you're trying to impress, someone you're not sure likes you, or someone you're afraid you might offend. STDs, which some people associate with promiscuity, are even more difficult to talk about. If teens have sex first and find out the sexual history of their partner afterward, it may then be too late to protect their sexual health.

POVERTY

People who live in poverty often cannot afford regular visits to a doctor. For this reason, even if they suspect they have an infection, they may not seek treatment. Some are suspicious of institutions, and so they stay away from health clinics that can provide information and treatment, even if those clinics are free.

RELIGIOUS AND CULTURAL TABOOS

Religious beliefs and traditions that discourage or condemn premarital sex, promiscuity, and adultery sometimes also discourage discussions of STDs. Many religions preach that because teens should avoid sexual behavior altogether, they do not need to know the facts about STDs and safe sex.

Some religious groups discourage the use of condoms (female or male condoms) because they believe that the use of birth control devices is wrong. They feel that humans do not have the right to interrupt the creation of another human life.

www.usatoday.com

News
SECTION A

October 4, 2010

From the Pages of USA TODAY

STD study revelation a reminder of era of abuses: Research like that sponsored by U.S. in Guatemala led to reforms

Susan Reverby describes three studies as the "trinity" of unholy medical research. Doctors at the Jewish Chronic Disease Hospital in New York City injected patients with live cancer cells. At Willowbrook State School, also in New York, researchers gave mentally disabled children hepatitis. In Tuskegee, Ala., doctors withheld treatment from black subjects to study the course of advanced syphilis.

Now there's a fourth.

On Friday, the U.S. government revealed that Reverby has unearthed a U.S.-sponsored study in Guatemala [in Central America], where doctors in the 1940s infected soldiers, prisoners, prostitutes and mental patients with syphilis and other sexually transmitted diseases. All traces of the study, which involved as many as 1,500 men and women, lay buried in a University of Pittsburgh [Pennsylvania] archive among the papers of researcher John Cutler of the U.S. Public Health Service. Cutler, who died in 2003, did syphilis research in Tuskegee.

The disclosure of what National Insti-tutes of Health Director Francis Collins called "a dark chapter" in medical history prompted President Obama to call Guatemalan President Alvaro Colom on Friday and apologize.

Cutler and his co-workers were trying to determine whether they could prevent syphilis with penicillin, a new drug in short supply between 1946 and 1948 when the studies were carried out. Hundreds of unwitting subjects were infected through cuts in their skin or through sex with prostitutes who had syphilis or were infected by researchers.

The Guatemalan government backed the trials, asking Cutler to "test and treat" men in army barracks and supply penicillin "as part of the price for cooperation," Reverby wrote in an article on the experiments scheduled to be published in January [2011] in the *Journal of Policy History*.

Cutler and his team decided to study prisoners in Guatemala City's Central Penitentiary [prison], because the men were allowed visits by prostitutes who could be used to infect them.

Reverby says the Guatemala experiments were carried out in secrecy by researchers who lied to their subjects and fretted that the program might be "wrecked" if it became public.

Reverby discovered the records of the Guatemala experiments when she was researching a book on the Tuskegee experiment, *Examining Tuskegee*, published in 2009. What struck her, she says, was that she has spent years trying to dispel a misconception that doctors were infecting the Tuskegee subjects with syphilis, yet here were documents showing that Cutler was infecting people, not in Tuskegee, but in Guatemala.

Still, the impact of Tuskegee continues to resonate, breeding distrust in minorities who often are reluctant to take part in research or seek medical care.

"We are concerned about the way in which this horrendous experiment, even though it was 60 years ago, may appear to people hearing about it today," Collins

Susan Reverby *(above)*, a medical historian at Wellesley College in Massachusetts, discovered records detailing secret STD experiments on people in Guatemala in the 1940s. The U.S. government conducted the medical study, with backing from the Guatemalan government.

says. "Today, the regulations that govern research by the U.S. government, whether funded domestically or internationally, would absolutely prohibit this kind of study."

—*Steve Sternberg*

In some cultural groups, women do not have the right to question their partner's sexual activities. They may not have the right to demand safe sex. These religious and cultural customs make the control of STDs more difficult. They also increase the risk that these infections will be passed from person to person.

MEDIA MESSAGES

Many people hesitate to talk about sex. Yet music, movies, television, and the Internet are filled with messages that sex is irresistible, trouble free, and fun. Characters in many TV shows think about sex, joke about sex, and have casual sexual encounters. They don't much worry about the physical consequences of their actions. In their storybook lives, they deal with romantic love and broken hearts. Yet they seldom if ever cope with the complications of an STD such as herpes or genital warts. The main message that comes across is that everyone is having sexual encounters, but nobody is worrying about the complications and responsibilities that go along with such encounters. Why should you? On the other hand, a few shows do tackle the complications of teen sexuality and the difficult decisions that many teens are making every day about their sexual lives.

MORE NUMEROUS SEXUAL CONTACTS

Americans in the twenty-first century tend to have multiple sexual contacts over the course of their lives. This applies to teens as well. Most sexually active teens describe themselves as monogamous. This means they are faithful to the person with whom they are having sex. However, their feelings and their relationships can change fairly rapidly. They might have several partners in the course of a relatively short period of time.

More sexual contact means there are more opportunities to transfer disease from one person to another. This is especially true when people do not take precautions to minimize the spread of STDs when they have casual sex. Many teens feel that sex should be a spontaneous, romantic, and passionate experience. They may feel guilty if they deliberately plan for it, or they may consider it promiscuous behavior to prepare for sex by carrying around a condom.

Also, although condoms are highly effective in preventing STDs, some people object to using them. If a woman's sexual partner (male or female) refuses to wear a condom, the woman can still protect herself by using the female condom. This is a sheath or a pouch—made of either polyurethane, synthetic nitrile, or latex—that is inserted into the vagina before sex. A variety of female condoms have been available since the 1990s. They have not, however, become a popular form of protection in the United States. Health-care practitioners and educators are working to change this by making teens aware of the female condom.

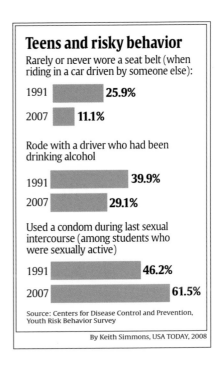

Teens and risky behavior

Rarely or never wore a seat belt (when riding in a car driven by someone else):

1991 **25.9%**
2007 **11.1%**

Rode with a driver who had been drinking alcohol

1991 **39.9%**
2007 **29.1%**

Used a condom during last sexual intercourse (among students who were sexually active)

1991 **46.2%**
2007 **61.5%**

Source: Centers for Disease Control and Prevention, Youth Risk Behavior Survey

By Keith Simmons, USA TODAY, 2008

MISPLACED TRUST

Teens often believe that trusting a boyfriend or a girlfriend is more important than asking questions and behaving carefully when it comes to sex. Trust can be misplaced, however. In at least one study, young men admitted that they lied about their sexual past. To convince a girl to have sex with them, they downplayed the number of their past partners. Or they didn't admit to having had an STD.

www.usatoday.com

USA TODAY

Life

SECTION D

November 23, 2010

From the Pages of USA TODAY

16, pregnant—and famous: MTV series, and their stars' celeb status, run risk of glamorizing teen motherhood

Maci Bookout, 19, wants to set the record straight.

She's still dating her boyfriend, Kyle King, 22. She's not house hunting in Hollywood, and she's not best friends with Taylor Swift. In fact, she has never spoken to her.

So who's Maci Bookout?

She's a teen mother and star of MTV reality show and ratings home run *Teen Mom*, which scored nearly 1.5 million more viewers this summer in its second-season premiere than the season finale of Emmy darling *Mad Men* last month.

Saturday Night Live has spoofed it. *Today* co-hosts Hoda Kotb and Kathie Lee Gifford have debated it. The Vatican's newspaper [the Vatican is the head-quarters of the Roman Catholic Church], *L'Osservatore Romano*, has written about MTV's pregnant programming.

The stories and personalities behind the pop-culture phenomenon are a casting director's dream.

Bookout, a sophomore at Chattanooga State Community College in Tennessee, gave birth to Bentley, now 2, when she was 17. She has a drama-filled relationship with Bentley's father, ex-boyfriend Ryan Edwards, 22. Marine City, Mich., native Catelynn Lowell, 18, gave birth to Carly, now 18 months, when she was 17 and decided with her fiance, Tyler Baltierra, 18, to put the baby up for an open adoption. Their adoption counselor helped the couple try out for *16 and Pregnant* [another MTV reality show].

Council Bluffs, Iowa, mom Farrah Abraham, 19, dreams of going to culinary school but for now is caring for Sophia, 21 months, whose 18-year-old father, Derek Underwood, died in a car accident months before she was born. Amber Portwood, 20, has made news in her hometown of Anderson, Ind., where on Thursday police charged her with two counts of felony domestic battery after they said she struck former fiance Gary Shirley, 24, on camera in front of their daughter, Leah, 2.

All four women are mainstays on USA

TODAY's Celebrity Heat Index, which measures media exposure; Portwood topped the list for October, beating out Angelina Jolie and Prince William. The moms are regularly on the covers of *People* and *Us Weekly* and have Facebook fan pages dedicated to them.

All of the attention prompts the question of whether the young women's rise to pop prominence glamorizes teen pregnancy and motherhood, says child psychologist Laurie Zelinger.

"While a teenage parent may be doing the best they can, they don't have all the information to weigh their options. The emotional part of them says, 'Wow, this is exciting getting my 15 minutes of fame,' but they're not always thinking of the effect on the child," she says. "I think it does increase the likelihood that for some people, they will say, 'I can do it, too.'"

While the *Teen Mom* stars have their share of struggles on the small screen each week, paparazzi [photographer] shots and tabloid covers manage to rip them out of the context of MTV and place them in the realm of celebrity, says *Teen Mom* executive producer Morgan J. Freeman.

"We stumbled into this current success of *Teen Mom* that is driven by a completely different industry. It's driven by a tabloid industry—the modern cultural-Twitter-online-viral monster that is outside of our control," he says. "[I'm] a little bit speechless that this show has kind of hit that pop phenom. Frankly, it's a challenge to stay focused on the real issues, stay focused on the real challenges in all of our girls' lives with this sort of larger cloud of the tabloids, the media circus, the glamorizing and glorifying aspects of it."

What they're trying to do, Freeman contends, is spread the message of teen pregnancy prevention and safe sex with the help of the four girls whose up-and-down lives show what he and MTV general manager Stephen Friedman describe as an "unvarnished" look.

"I'm not trying to glamorize teen pregnancy," says Lowell, who adds that she and Baltierra regularly communicate with Carly's adoptive parents. "If anything, I'm trying to stop it or at least try to make [teens] make better decisions like using protection or birth control. I'm doing the show for a good reason—to show teens that these are struggles that you go through when you become a young mom."

Bookout concedes that all of the attention is "weird" for her and Bentley but says that the larger picture is more important.

"I don't think I would ever regret doing *16 and Pregnant* or *Teen Mom* because I did it for educational reasons," she says. "I definitely think it's doing its job, because some of the feedback I get from younger girls is really good as far as, 'I'm going to wait to have sex' or 'I'm going to use safe sex.' That was my goal. I didn't do it for the fame or for the attention."

—Arienne Thompson

Some even said that they would lie to a potential sexual partner. They might tell that person that they had been tested for HIV/AIDS, when they hadn't, in order to have sex.

ALCOHOL AND DRUGS

Alcohol and drug use often leads to risky sexual behavior that can put teens at high risk for STDs. One study of more than thirty-four thousand teens found that those who drank were seven times more likely to have sex than their peers who abstained from alcohol. Teens under fifteen who used drugs were almost four times more likely to have sex than those who did not use drugs.

Under the influence of alcohol and drugs, sexual encounters are often casual, unplanned, and unprotected. Since drinkers may have impaired judgment, they are less likely to worry about STDs or safe sex.

Teenagers under the influence of alcohol often have unplanned and unprotected sexual encounters.

DENIAL

Despite the rising numbers of teens contracting HIV/AIDS in the United States, many teens do not believe that they will catch HIV or any other STD. Because of well-publicized, effective new treatments, some teens believe, incorrectly, that HIV/AIDS is now curable. They might think they are not old enough or promiscuous enough to become infected. Or they might think that STDs strike only certain groups of people, such as homosexuals, prostitutes, the poor, or people in other countries. Following the same logic of those who smoke or who don't wear seat belts, some teens mistakenly assume that nothing bad can ever happen to them.

I'M INFECTED WHERE?

Another reason that STDs impact adults and teens is that the diseases affect a portion of the human body—the reproductive organs, or genitals—that is considered very personal and private. Many people do not regularly examine their genitals. For this reason, they may fail to discover a telltale blister or sore. If they notice a symptom, they may ignore it and hope it will go away rather than face an examination by a doctor.

It is often easier to discuss a problem if you know the terminology to use. The following section will help you gain some familiarity with terms that describe parts of the male and female reproductive systems. These terms will help you in later discussions of symptoms and complications of STDs.

THE MALE REPRODUCTIVE SYSTEM

Most male reproductive organs are located outside the body. A primary organ, the penis, is a tube-shaped structure through

USA TODAY

which runs a smaller tube called the urethra. The urethra serves a dual purpose: it carries urine from the bladder and sperm (male reproductive cells) from the testicles. When a male is sexually excited or aroused, the penis becomes large and stiff so that it can be easily inserted into a female's vagina.

Two other primary male reproductive organs, the testicles, lie behind and below the penis. They are egg-shaped and encased in a loose sac of skin called the scrotum. The testicles produce testosterone, a male hormone, as well as sperm. Small tubules known as the epididymis and the vas deferens carry sperm from the testicles to the urethra. During ejaculation, sperm are transported out of the penis in semen. This fluid is produced by the prostate gland and the seminal vesicles, both of which are located inside the body, near the bladder and in front of the large intestine.

The anus is the body's intestinal opening. In a man, it is behind the testicles and the scrotum and between the buttocks. It is not technically part of the male reproductive system but can sometimes be affected by sexually transmitted diseases.

THE FEMALE REPRODUCTIVE SYSTEM

Many of the female reproductive organs are located inside the body. The uterus is a muscular, pear-shaped organ that lies in the lower abdomen between the bladder and the large intestine. During pregnancy, the uterus stretches to allow for the growth of the baby inside. The lower end of the uterus is called the cervix. Set to either side of the uterus are the ovaries, where eggs (female reproductive cells) and estrogen, a female hormone, are produced. Partially encircling the ovaries are the fallopian tubes, through which a mature egg travels on its way to the uterus. The uterus opens into the vagina, through which semen passes to the ovaries during heterosexual sex.

MALE REPRODUCTIVE SYSTEM

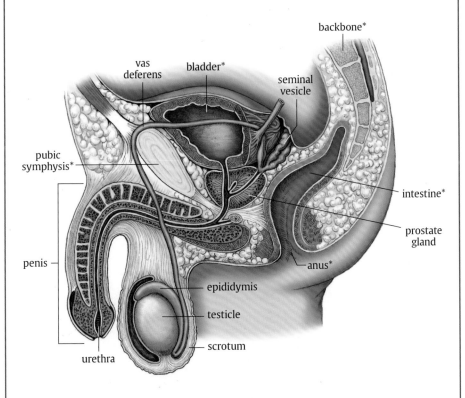

*not part of the male reproductive system

During birth, a baby passes to the outside of the mother's body through the vagina. An external reproductive structure in the female is the vulva, which consists of the inner and outer labia, fleshy folds of skin. The clitoris, the organ of female sexual arousal, is about the size of a raisin and sits above the vaginal opening.

The urethra, through which urine passes from the bladder, is not part of the reproductive system in the female. The urethra is an internal organ that ends in a tiny opening between the clitoris and the vagina. In women, the anus lies below the vulva and between the buttocks. As in the male, both the urethra and the anus can be affected by STDs.

RATE YOUR RISK

To better understand if you are at risk for catching an STD, answer the following questions. Then tally your score to see if you are taking risks with your health and your future.

1. Have you ever had sexual intercourse?
   ❏ yes (2 pts)   ❏ no (0 pts)
   If you abstain from (do not have) sexual intercourse, you are at low risk of catching an STD.

   Do not answer the following if you answered NO to question #1.
2. Do you ever have sex without using a condom?
   ❏ yes (2 pts)   ❏ no (1 pt)
   Not using a condom every time you have sex puts you at high risk for catching an STD.

3. Have you or your sexual partner ever shared needles while using intravenous drugs (drugs injected into a vein)?
   ❏ yes (15 pts)   ❏ no (0 pts)

FEMALE REPRODUCTIVE SYSTEM

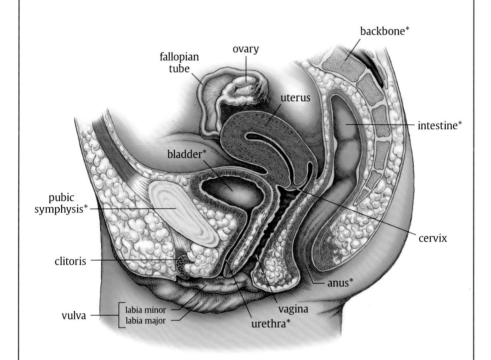

*not part of the female reproductive system

Sharing needles or having sex with someone who uses intravenous drugs greatly increases your risk of contracting HIV/AIDS and hepatitis B.

4. Do you have sex during or after using drugs or alcohol?
   ❏ yes (2 pts)   ❏ no (1 pt)
   Having sex while drinking or using drugs lowers your inhibitions and can lead to taking unsafe sexual risks.

5. Do you have sex with people you don't know well or don't know at all?
   ❏ yes (2 pts)   ❏ no (1 pt)
   It can be very dangerous to your health to have sex with someone you don't know and whose sexual past is unknown to you.

6. Do you know or think that your partner has had sex with other partners?
   ❏ yes (2 pts)   ❏ no (1 pt)
   When you have sex with someone, you don't only risk catching an STD from that person. Through sex with him or her, you are also exposed to any STDs carried by that person's former partners.

7. Have you had sex with more than one partner in the last three months?
   ❏ yes (2 pts)   ❏ no (1 pt)
   Every time you have sex with a new partner, you raise the odds that you could catch an STD. This is because each new partner brings a sexual history with him or her. Some of that history may be unhealthy sexual practices that put you at risk too.

8. Have you ever had sex with someone in exchange for money or drugs?

   ❑ yes (2 pts)   ❑ no (1 pt)

   Having sex for drugs or money is very risky behavior. Sexual partners who offer money or drugs in exchange for sex are risk takers. They are more likely to have had unprotected sex with many partners, including prostitutes.

9. Are you . . .

   ❑ male (1 pt)

   ❑ female (2 pts)?

   Due to anatomical differences, females are at greater risk of catching STDs than men.

10. Are you . . .

   ❑ under 25 years old (2 pts)

   ❑ 25 or older (1 pt)?

   People under the age of twenty-five are at greater risk for catching STDs than people who are older than that.

If your total is below 10, your behavior puts you at little or no risk of catching an STD. If your score is from 10 to 14, you have some risk of catching an STD. If you score above 14, some aspects of your behavior are putting you at high risk for catching an STD.

No matter what your risk level, it is wise to be well informed about STDs. You should know how to recognize symptoms (if any) and to understand what to do if you suspect you're infected. This book presents information on the seven most common and health-threatening STDs in the United States. These are chlamydia, gonorrhea, syphilis, genital herpes, HIV/AIDS, genital warts, and hepatitis B.

CHAPTER TWO

WHAT YOU SHOULD KNOW
ABOUT CHLAMYDIA

Nakeesha's pelvic inflammatory disease stemmed from her primary health issue—chlamydia. This is a common STD among young, sexually active women.

Because she was pregnant, Nakeesha was hospitalized and treated with antibiotics. When Sergio came to visit her, she told him that he, too, needed to be tested for chlamydia. Sergio had no symptoms and felt fine. Although he didn't want to be tested, the doctor insisted. To Sergio's surprise, his test was also positive for chlamydia.

Now recovered, Nakeesha thinks back on her infection. Having been with no one but Sergio, she knows that she got chlamydia from him and wonders how he caught a sexually transmitted disease. She would like to talk to him about it, but doesn't think she can. Sergio says that many of his friends have had clap (gonorrhea) before, and that dealing with chlamydia or gonorrhea is not a big deal. Nakeesha hopes this is true. Still, she worries that Sergio is not being faithful, and that she may become infected with something more serious next time.

WHAT IS CHLAMYDIA?

Chlamydia was first recognized as an STD by medical experts in about 1970. At the start of the twenty-first

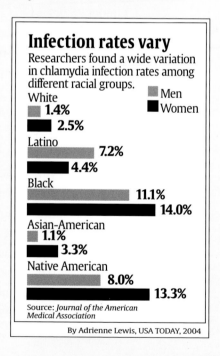

Infection rates vary

Researchers found a wide variation in chlamydia infection rates among different racial groups.

Men
Women

White
1.4%
2.5%

Latino
7.2%
4.4%

Black
11.1%
14.0%

Asian-American
1.1%
3.3%

Native American
8.0%
13.3%

Source: *Journal of the American Medical Association*

By Adrienne Lewis, USA TODAY, 2004

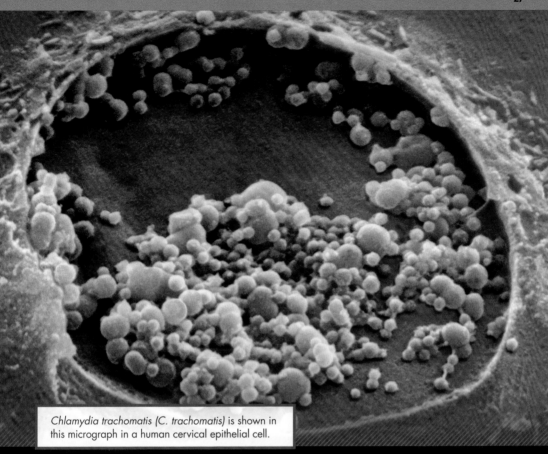

Chlamydia trachomatis (C. trachomatis) is shown in this micrograph in a human cervical epithelial cell.

century, it was the most common, fastest-spreading, nonviral STD in the United States. Caused by a tiny bacteria, *Chlamydia trachomatis* (*C. trachomatis*), chlamydia can infect the urinary-genital area; the anal area; and sometimes the eyes, the throat, and the lungs.

In 2009 more than 1.2 million new cases of chlamydia were reported to the Centers for Disease Control and Prevention (CDC), the top public health agency in the United States. Because a large number of people do not know they have chlamydia, however, the agency estimates that the number of those infected annually is closer to 2.8 million. Various studies show that up to 50 percent of symptom-free individuals who are randomly tested for chlamydia test positive for the bacteria.

www.usatoday.com

USA TODAY

Life

SECTION D

November 14, 2007

From the Pages of USA TODAY

Chlamydia cases top 1M, while STDs rise slightly overall

Federal officials report that chlamydia cases reported in the USA have topped 1 million for the first time, with the highest rates among adolescent girls. The growing prevalence of chlamydia, which can cause pelvic inflammatory disease and infertility, is mirrored by parallel increases in the prevalence of gonorrhea and syphilis after years of declines.

While STD clinics report new cases, experts say, private doctors often don't. "We have reason to believe that chlamydia is dramatically underreported," says John Douglas, director of STD prevention at CDC in Atlanta [Georgia].

Frequently a silent infection that doesn't produce symptoms, chlamydia's impact may not be felt for years, says gynecologist [a doctor specializing in the female reproductive system] Kevin Ault of the Emory University Woodruff Health Sciences Center in Atlanta. "I often tell patients that chlamydia's a stealth bomber," he says. "You have it when you're 19 and don't know it. Ten years later, when you're trying to conceive a child, you have damaged fallopian tubes."

Doctors say efforts to fight STDs have been hampered by pressure to respond to a range of public health problems, from AIDS to emerging infectious diseases to food-borne epidemics. "The gap between what we were previously able to do and what we need to do is growing larger," Douglas says.

The diminishing number of people with health insurance makes matters worse, Douglas says. "If you don't have insurance, you're unlikely to get care," he says, adding that untreated STD patients are more likely to infect others.

—Steve Sternberg

Anyone who has ever had more than one sexual partner or has a new sexual partner or fails to use condoms regularly and/or has a gonorrhea infection is at high risk for chlamydia. The highest rates of infection are among female teens. This seems to be because the tissue of the teen cervix is thinner than the adult cervix and is therefore more vulnerable to infection. Experts estimate that one out of every ten teenage girls in the United States may be infected with chlamydia.

HOW IS CHLAMYDIA TRANSMITTED?

Chlamydia is easy to transmit through oral, genital, or anal sex with an infected partner. The bacteria are carried in semen and vaginal fluids. Chlamydia primarily infects the mucous membranes of the cervix in women and of the urethra in men. It can also infect other mucous membranes as well.

Chlamydia can be passed from mother to baby as the baby passes through the birth canal. About 50 percent of babies born to infected mothers acquire chlamydial eye infections, and about 10 percent develop lung infections. For infants, such infections can lead to blindness, permanent lung damage, or death from pneumonia.

Kissing is not a risk factor in transmitting chlamydia. Infection is also not passed on towels, toilet seats, bedding, or other inanimate objects.

WHAT ARE THE SYMPTOMS OF CHLAMYDIA?

People often experience no symptoms when they are infected with chlamydia. One-half of infected men and three-quarters of infected women are completely symptom free. They are usually surprised when they are told they have tested positive for chlamydia. A person can be symptom free for life, or symptoms can develop weeks, months, or years after infection takes place.

For those individuals who do have symptoms, these are usually mild. Women may experience a frequent need to urinate, burning during urination, genital irritation, and yellowish-green vaginal discharge. In males, symptoms include a clear, thin discharge from the penis; burning with urination; an itchy or irritated feeling in the urethra; and redness at the tip of the penis. In both males and females, symptoms usually disappear about three weeks after exposure.

Chlamydial eye infections produce conjunctivitis—redness, itching, and pain in the eyes. With infections of the anal area, symptoms may include pain, discharge, and bleeding. Chlamydia of the throat, contracted during oral sex, may produce no symptoms or may appear as a sore throat.

ARE THERE COMPLICATIONS FROM CHLAMYDIA?

Serious complications can arise when a chlamydia infection goes untreated. In men this can include infection of the prostate gland. It can also lead to epididymitis—a medical condition involving inflammation of the epididymis. Scarring in this part of the testicle can result in infertility. (Infertility is the inability of a man to make a woman pregnant or of a woman to become pregnant.) In women, infection can and often does spread to the uterus, fallopian tubes, and ovaries, developing into pelvic inflammatory disease. Scarring from PID can lead to infertility or to ectopic pregnancies. Ectopic pregnancy, in which a fertilized egg implants in the fallopian tubes instead of in the lining of the uterus, can lead to pain, significant bleeding, and even death.

A person can become infected with chlamydia repeatedly. Recurrent chlamydial infections usually are more severe, with greater likelihood of pelvic inflammatory disease. With each episode of PID, a woman has a 20 percent reduction in her chances of having children, as well as a 20 percent increased chance of chronic pelvic pain and ectopic pregnancy.

Reiter's syndrome is a rare complication that occurs in some people with chlamydia. This condition involves recurrent episodes of urethritis (infection of the urethra), arthritis, conjunctivitis, skin rashes, and other symptoms. Reiter's syndrome may recur even after the infection has been treated with antibiotics. It seems to be the body's mistaken attempt to fight off infection by attacking healthy tissues. Experts are unsure why some people develop Reiter's syndrome. They believe there may be a genetic predisposition for the condition.

HOW DOES A DOCTOR DIAGNOSE CHLAMYDIA?

Testing for chlamydia is not a routine part of a regular physical checkup. A doctor may not think to suggest that a teen have a diagnostic test. Often the first time a woman is diagnosed as having had chlamydia is when she cannot become pregnant later in life, after scarring of the fallopian tubes has taken place.

Once a person decides to be tested for chlamydia, several procedures are available. A health-care provider can help decide which procedure is the best for each individual. The culture method involves a doctor taking a swab of material from the cervix or a small swab of fluid from the penis. The sample is cultured (allowed to grow) in a nutrient solution in a lab. Lab technicians then look for bacteria under a microscope. Culture tests are also used to diagnose chlamydial throat and anal infections.

A doctor may also take a blood or urine sample and order non-culture tests. These tests include the enzyme-linked immunosorbent assay (ELISA) and the polymerase chain reaction

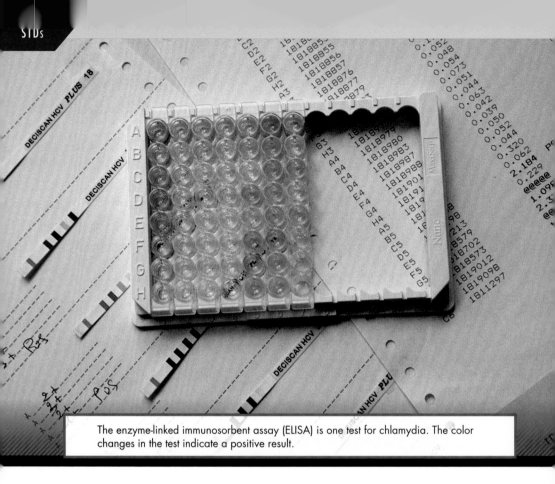

The enzyme-linked immunosorbent assay (ELISA) is one test for chlamydia. The color changes in the test indicate a positive result.

(PCR). Both look directly for bacterial genetic material. Although more accurate than culture tests, ELISA and PCR tests are also more expensive.

WHAT IS THE TREATMENT FOR CHLAMYDIA?

Once diagnosed, chlamydia can be cured with antibiotic treatment. For an uncomplicated infection, doctors will commonly prescribe a short course of an antibiotic such as azithromycin, doxycycline, or erythromycin. With PID or infection of the epididymis or prostate, a longer course of medication is usually necessary. Although antibiotics can kill all chlamydia bacteria, they cannot reverse the aftereffects of PID such as scarring and chronic pain.

Erythromycin is usually prescribed for pregnant women who are infected with chlamydia, since other antibiotics may be harmful to the unborn child. When a mother is treated, the baby faces almost no risk of being born with chlamydia. To help ensure that newborns do not develop chlamydial eye infections, hospitals routinely treat all babies' eyes with antibiotic ointment shortly after birth.

Until a physician determines that an individual is free of chlamydia infection, all sexual contact should be avoided. It is important that all of an infected person's partners be checked and treated for chlamydia, whether or not they have symptoms. (In many states, it is mandatory to report chlamydia infections to the state health department.) Follow-up testing is important for all involved to ensure that the infection has disappeared completely.

CHAPTER THREE

WHAT YOU SHOULD KNOW ABOUT GONORRHEA AND SYPHILIS

Celeste knew that other girls sometimes had sex at parties, but she never thought that she'd be one of them. Her first sexual encounter wasn't as romantic as she'd thought it would be. She was embarrassed afterward that she'd become intimate with Kurtis, whom she didn't know well.

Celeste was not going to easily forget the incident, however. When she went to her family doctor for a sports physical in late July, she mentioned to the doctor that she was having pain and itching when she urinated. She was also spotting between her periods. The doctor did a pelvic exam and took a swab from her cervix. The sample showed that Celeste was infected with gonorrhea.

The discovery left Celeste shaken. Although the doctor was professional and nonjudgmental, the prescription to cure her STD couldn't be kept from her parents. When they found out what had happened, they were furious with Kurtis and disappointed in their daughter. Cases of gonorrhea must be reported to the state health department. Celeste therefore also had to tell the doctor that Kurtis was the one who gave her the disease.

WHAT IS GONORRHEA?

Gonorrhea is another very common STD in the United States. It is caused by the bacterium *Neisseria gonorrhoeae* (*N. gonorrhoeae*), which produces a number of genital infections and can also infect the mouth, the throat, and the anal area.

More than 350,000 cases of gonorrhea were reported to the CDC in 2006. Some experts estimate that the number of actual cases may be more than twice as high, however. Infection rates are dropping for adults, but they are rising for teens and for people from twenty to twenty-four. Sexually active teens living in high-density urban areas are at greatest risk, but anyone who has multiple partners, engages in unprotected sex, or both can catch gonorrhea.

HOW IS GONORRHEA TRANSMITTED?

Gonorrhea is very easy to catch. It is transmitted through sexual contact with an infected partner and through oral sex. The bacteria are carried in infected discharge, semen, and vaginal fluids. Gonorrhea commonly infects the mucous membranes of the urethra in males and the cervix in females, although other mucous membranes can be

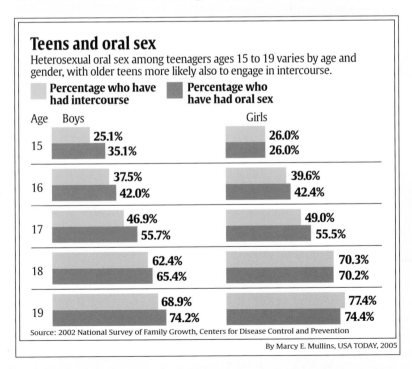

Teens and oral sex

Heterosexual oral sex among teenagers ages 15 to 19 varies by age and gender, with older teens more likely also to engage in intercourse.

Percentage who have had intercourse **Percentage who have had oral sex**

Age	Boys		Girls	
15	25.1%	35.1%	26.0%	26.0%
16	37.5%	42.0%	39.6%	42.4%
17	46.9%	55.7%	49.0%	55.5%
18	62.4%	65.4%	70.3%	70.2%
19	68.9%	74.2%	77.4%	74.4%

Source: 2002 National Survey of Family Growth, Centers for Disease Control and Prevention

By Marcy E. Mullins, USA TODAY, 2005

USA TODAY

infected as well. Anyone who is sexually active can be infected. The CDC, however, states that the highest rate of infection is reported in teenagers. Gonorrhea can be passed from an infected woman to her infant during delivery, but it cannot be passed by contact with inanimate objects such as toilet seats and towels.

WHAT ARE THE SYMPTOMS OF GONORRHEA?

About 10 percent of men and more than 50 percent of women have no symptoms when they catch gonorrhea. For those who do experience symptoms, these usually develop within two to ten days of sexual contact with an infected partner. A few people may experience symptoms as early as one day after infection, while some may feel nothing for several weeks.

In a female, symptoms of gonorrhea may include pain or burning during urination, yellow or bloody vaginal discharge, or spotting between menstrual periods and after intercourse. In males, the most common symptom is discharge from the penis and a moderate to severe burning sensation during urination. Discharge is usually yellow and heavy, although it can be clear and almost unnoticeable.

Both men and women can experience gonorrheal infection in the rectal area, contracted through anal sex. Symptoms include rectal pain, itching, discharge, and bleeding. Gonorrhea of the throat, contracted during oral sex, may produce no symptoms or may be experienced as a sore throat. Redness and a thick yellow discharge mark a gonorrheal eye infection, most common in newborns.

ARE THERE COMPLICATIONS FROM GONORRHEA?

Complications that can develop from gonorrhea are usually painful and more serious than the initial infection. As with chlamydia, gonorrhea infection in women can develop into pelvic inflammatory disease. Gonorrhea can also infect the abdominal area and cause pain and inflammation around the liver, a condition known as Fitz-Hugh-Curtis syndrome. Women who become infected with gonorrhea while they are pregnant run a risk of miscarriage and premature delivery.

In men, complications of gonorrhea can include infection of the prostate, which causes pain between the testicles and the anal area. If the epididymis becomes infected, scarring can cause infertility.

Very rarely, gonorrhea can spread through the bloodstream to other parts of the body. This can cause a more serious and, in rare cases, fatal disease called disseminated gonococcal infection (DGI). Symptoms of this condition include fever, chills, joint pain, rashes, endocarditis (infection of the heart valves), and meningitis (infection of the lining of the brain and spinal cord).

HOW DOES A DOCTOR DIAGNOSE GONORRHEA?

Testing for gonorrhea must always involve a doctor's examination. For males, the doctor will commonly use the Gram's stain test, during which a sample of discharge is taken from the urethra, placed on a slide, and stained with dye. Lab technicians then examine the slide under a microscope for the presence of bacteria. For females, culture tests may give more accurate results. In these tests, a sample of discharge from the urethra or the cervix is brushed across a nutrient medium. Lab technicians allow the culture to grow for forty-eight hours and then examine it under the microscope. For this test to be successful in diagnosing the presence or absence of gonorrhea, the doctor must be sure to gather enough bacteria on the swab to culture.

Because microscopic examinations sometimes miss infections, doctors are more likely to use more sensitive procedures to detect the genes of the bacteria. These procedures are usually more accurate, but they can be more expensive.

WHAT IS THE TREATMENT FOR GONORRHEA?

Gonorrhea can readily be cured with antibiotics. For years penicillin was the drug of choice, but cases of resistant bacteria (that is, bacteria that are not killed by penicillin and other antibiotics) have become more common over time. Patients are often given a single dose injection of ceftriaxone or a single oral dose of cefixime. For more complicated infections such as PID or endocarditis, hospitalization and a longer course of antibiotic treatment may be necessary.

In most states, gonorrhea must be reported to the state health department to ensure that all sexual partners of the infected person are contacted and receive treatment. A follow-up examination of all parties is important to ensure that treatment has been fully effective.

WHAT IS SYPHILIS?

Syphilis is caused by the bacterium *Treponema pallidum* (*T. pallidum*). Because of its spiral shape, the bacterium is called a spirochete. Known as the great imitator, syphilis can mimic a variety of diseases and can affect virtually every part of the body.

Far less prevalent than gonorrhea, just over thirty-six thousand new cases of syphilis were reported to the CDC in the United States in 2006. Teens should not dismiss the disease as irrelevant to their lives, however. Rates of syphilis remain high in some regions of the United States. In these areas, poverty, lack of education, and inadequate access to health care contribute to higher rates of infection.

April 13, 2007

From the Pages of USA TODAY

Gonorrhea mutates to resist antibiotic treatment; Development is 'a public health wake-up call,' CDC official warns

Gonorrhea has become so resistant to one class of antibiotics that the Centers for Disease Control and Prevention (CDC) announced that those drugs should no longer be used to treat it.

Now that fluoroquinolones, such as Cipro, are no longer recommended, only a single class of antibiotics, called cephalosporins, is left to treat gonorrhea, the second-most common infectious disease reported to the CDC. The last gonorrhea treatment to be dropped because of antibiotic resistance was penicillin in the 1980s, said John Douglas, director of the CDC's Division of Sexually Transmitted Diseases Prevention. "This is not doomsday, but it is a public health wake-up call," he said.

Fluoroquinolones are widely used because they are effective against a range of bacteria and fewer people are allergic to them than to other antibiotics. Apparently, Douglas said, it's easier for bacteria to mutate and resist fluoroquinolones than it is for them to become resistant to cephalosporins.

"Gonorrhea has now joined the list of other superbugs for which treatment options have become dangerously few," Henry Masur, president of the Infectious Diseases Society of America, told the Associated Press. "To make a bad problem even worse, we're also seeing a decline in the development of new antibiotics to treat these infections."

Overall in men, 13.3% of gonorrhea cases were resistant to fluoroquinolones in the first half of 2006, compared with fewer than 1% in 2001. A higher dose might cure some of those cases, Douglas said, but that gets costly and may still be ineffective against the most resistant bacteria.

Most infected women don't develop symptoms, and many clear gonorrhea [get rid of the infection] with no treatment. However, a significant proportion of infected women develop pelvic inflammatory disease, which can lead to infertility. In rare cases in men, he said, gonorrhea can cause upper genital tract infections that can leave them sterile.

—*Rita Rubin*

HOW IS SYPHILIS TRANSMITTED?

Like gonorrhea, syphilis is transmitted through sexual contact—vaginal, oral, or anal—with an infected partner. Sources of infection are syphilitic sores, rashes, and lesions, and possibly blood, semen, and vaginal secretions. Bacteria enter an uninfected person's body by passing through mucous membranes or through tiny breaks in the skin. The microbes are easily transmitted. On average, a person has a one in three chance of contracting syphilis from a single unprotected sexual contact with an infected person. There is no evidence that syphilis is passed on toilet seats, swimming pools, hot tubs, bathtubs, shared clothing, or other inanimate objects.

During an infected woman's pregnancy, syphilis often crosses the placental barrier and infects a fetus. (The placental barrier is made up of the tissues that protect the fetus by separating its blood from the mother's blood.) Results of such infection can be very serious. Almost half of untreated infected women will have a stillbirth (a baby that is dead at birth) or will deliver a baby that dies shortly after birth. Babies who survive have up to a 70 percent chance of having congenital syphilis (syphilis existing at or before birth).

WHAT ARE THE SYMPTOMS OF SYPHILIS?

Syphilic infection is divided into early and late stages. Symptoms vary depending on the stage.

The early stage of syphilis includes primary, secondary, and early latent periods. Primary syphilis starts at the moment of infection and lasts for several months. The first symptom is a single, painless sore called a chancre. The chancre is small and round with raised edges. It appears between ten and ninety days (the average is three weeks) after infection at the point where the bacterium entered the body.

This can be the penis or scrotum in males; the vagina in females; or the anus, lips, or tongue in either sex.

Many people miss the initial chancre because it is painless and is often in a nonvisible spot. Swollen lymph nodes in the genital area may signal that something is wrong, but these are painless as well and can go unnoticed. Symptoms usually disappear without treatment after a few weeks. The infected person may never know he or she has syphilis.

Without treatment, secondary syphilis develops. During this period, bacteria enter the bloodstream and spread to other organs in the body. Persons are extremely infectious to sexual partners at this stage. They can even infect others through nonsexual contact, such as through a break in the skin. Symptoms may be similar to the flu and can also include:

- A rash characterized by brown sores, particularly on the palms of the hands and the soles of the feet
- Swollen lymph nodes (anywhere in the body)
- Sore throat
- Joint pain
- Headache and fever
- Hair loss
- Wartlike lesions in the genital area

If the disease is not treated at this point, symptoms again disappear, and early latent syphilis begins. This period can last for decades and can be detected only through blood tests. During this time, however, spirochetes multiply and spread into the circulatory system, central nervous system, brain, and bones. A person with syphilis is commonly not infectious during this period.

Late stage, or tertiary, syphilis is rarely seen in the twenty-first century. First, many people get treatment earlier in their infection.

Second, 75 percent of people with long-term syphilis remain in the latent stage. They never show symptoms or progress to the next stage of the disease. If symptoms do occur, however, they are extremely serious. Tertiary syphilis can damage almost any organ or system in the body. Neurosyphilis, infection of the nervous system, can cause progressive paralysis. Other symptoms include dementia (a loss of mental capabilities), blindness, degeneration of the body's reflexes, vomiting, deep sores on the soles of the feet, and severe abdominal pain. Death can occur due to infection of the heart and major blood vessels.

Some children who are born with syphilis may have no symptoms. Others may have a variety of problems that include failure to gain weight, fever, rashes, sores, bone lesions, and bone deformities. Complications such as deafness, blindness, bone pain, and deterioration of the central nervous system may appear later in the lives of children born with syphilis. Some typical, irreversible signs that a child has had congenital syphilis include physical abnormalities such as a high forehead; the absence of the upper, bony part of the nose (saddlenose); and peg-shaped teeth (Hutchinson's teeth).

HOW DOES A DOCTOR DIAGNOSE SYPHILIS?

Medical professionals have several methods of diagnosing syphilis. A doctor may recognize physical symptoms such as a chancre. He or she may choose to swab lesions to obtain bacteria, which can then be identified with a microscope. Or the doctor can choose instead to draw a blood sample and order blood tests. The most common blood tests are the venereal disease research laboratory (VDRL) test and the rapid plasma reagin (RPR) test. Such tests will show a positive reaction within a few weeks of infection and will continue to do so unless an infected person receives treatment. These tests sometimes produce inaccurate results. For that reason, the doctor may order a follow-up test, commonly the fluorescent treponemal antibody absorption (FTA-ABS) test. This test is accurate in 70 to 90 percent of cases.

In many areas of the world, including parts of the United States, it is common for pregnant women to be tested for syphilis during a routine prenatal checkup. If an infected woman is treated during the first four months of her pregnancy, the unborn baby is very unlikely to be infected with syphilis.

WHAT IS THE TREATMENT FOR SYPHILIS?

Most cases of syphilis, including congenital syphilis, can be cured with penicillin. However, any damage to body organs and systems cannot be reversed. In persons who have had an infection for less than a year, a single injection of penicillin is usually sufficient. For long-term infections or for persons with neurosyphilis, a series of penicillin injections is necessary. Persons who are allergic to penicillin can be treated with other antibiotics. For pregnant women and infants with syphilis, a specialist should oversee the course of treatment.

In all cases, follow-up blood tests to ensure that the bacteria are totally eliminated from the body are essential, especially if a person is also infected with HIV. Sexual partners of an infected person must also be tested by a physician to determine their STD status and to prevent worsening of the infection or reinfection.

By law, new cases of syphilis must be reported to a state health department to ensure that all sexual partners are contacted and receive treatment. People do not develop immunity to gonorrhea and syphilis. So if a person has been infected with either disease before, he or she can become infected again and again. For that reason, periodic checkups are important.

CHAPTER FOUR

WHAT YOU SHOULD KNOW
ABOUT GENITAL HERPES

Leah has often shared her thoughts with her older sister Susan, and she has this time, too. Susan suggested that Leah get some information on birth control before she takes the next step. Both girls went to a health clinic in a nearby town. A nurse there informed Leah that birth control pills would prevent pregnancy but not sexually transmitted diseases. She gave Leah some brochures and complimentary condoms. She also suggested that both Leah and Daniel be tested for STDs before they go any further in their relationship.

Leah was embarrassed to talk to Daniel about condoms and STDs. She put it off for a few days. Finally, she wrote him a note explaining what the nurse had said and asking him what he thought.

The idea of using a condom bothered Daniel. He felt sex should be spontaneous and that using a condom would spoil the experience. Leah agreed to compromise. She promised that she would go on birth control pills—after all, neither of them wanted to start a family yet. She also would forget about using condoms if Daniel would go in and be tested for STDs. Daniel reluctantly agreed.

Both Daniel and Leah were astounded when Daniel tested positive for genital herpes. Daniel did remember having had some itchy blisters on his penis a year before. He told Leah not to worry, however, because the problem had gone away.

Leah is not convinced. She read the brochures and learned that genital herpes symptoms can come and go, but the infection remains. Daniel could still give her the disease. Daniel tells her that if she loves him, then his STD shouldn't come between them. Leah isn't sure what to think. She's worried about catching genital herpes, a disease that she would have for the rest of her life.

WHAT IS GENITAL HERPES?

Before HIV/AIDS, which was first noticed by the medical community in the early 1980s, genital herpes was the most feared STD because it was and still is incurable. In the twenty-first century, genital herpes remains a painful and disruptive part of many people's lives. Caused by the herpes simplex type 2 virus (HSV-2), it is one of a family of viruses that causes cold sores, chicken pox, shingles, and mononucleosis. Herpes simplex type 1 virus (HSV-1), which causes oral herpes (cold sores), is a close relative of HSV-2. Oral herpes most commonly occurs around the face and is transmitted nonsexually through kissing. Oral herpes can also appear on the hands of someone who touches a cold sore. HSV-1 can sometimes infect the genital area, however. HSV-2 commonly infects the genitals but can infect the face, the throat, and the eyes as well.

At the start of the twenty-first century, about five hundred thousand new cases of genital herpes were diagnosed in the United States each year. About one in six people in the United States between the ages of fourteen and forty-nine live with the virus. With no known cure for the disease, the number of people infected with the virus continues to rise. The chance of catching genital herpes during a single sexual encounter with a partner who is infectious is very high—about 50 percent for men and 80 to 90 percent for women.

Teens and young adults are at high risk for genital herpes because they tend to have more short-term sexual relationships with a number of different partners. In the year 2000, genital herpes infections were five times more frequent among white teens than they were in the 1980s. A CDC study for the years 2005 to 2008 found that among the general population, women were twice as likely to be infected as men. Additionally, the prevalence of the disease was three times greater among African Americans than among whites.

July 20, 2010

From the Pages of USA TODAY

Anti-HIV gel is declared breakthrough for women; Risk of genital herpes also sharply reduced

Researchers say they've achieved the first AIDS prevention breakthrough for women. More than a decade of failure and frustration ended with a report that a new vaginal gel gives women the power to reduce their risk of contracting HIV and genital herpes without relying on their male partner to use a condom.

The experimental gel is made with Gilead Sciences' antiviral drug tenofovir, which is widely used for treating HIV, the virus that causes AIDS. Applying the 1% tenofovir gel 12 hours before and 12 hours after sex reduced a woman's risk of HIV infection by 39% over the course of 2 -1/2 years. The gel also reduced the risk of genital herpes by 51%, an unexpected bonus because women with herpes are twice as likely to be infected with HIV.

At this level of protection, the researchers say, widespread use of the gel could prevent 1.3 million infections and more than 800,000 deaths in South Africa alone over the next 20 years. Researchers and advocates who have grown accustomed to failure, or worse—one promising vaginal gel actually was found to boost the risk of infection—hailed the report.

"This is good news," says Yasmin Halima, director of the Global Campaign for Microbicides, an advocacy group that has championed the approach. "Women are vulnerable to HIV across the world. Just having condoms for men is not really a viable option."

In the study, 889 sexually active women ages 18 to 40 were given either the tenofovir gel or a placebo (an inactive substance used for experiments). Of 434 women who did not have herpes at the start of the trial, 29 of those using tenofovir became infected vs. 58 using a placebo. The gel worked best in the women who used it most consistently. Anthony Fauci, director of the National Institute for Allergy and Infectious Diseases, says the study marks a "significant conceptual advance" in efforts to give women the tools they need to protect themselves.

"The level of protection isn't as high as we hoped it would be," Fauci says, "but there are a lot of things we can do to change that. The degree of the effect was related to the degree (to which women used the gel.)"

—*Steve Sternberg*

HOW IS GENITAL HERPES TRANSMITTED?

Genital herpes can easily be transmitted through unprotected vaginal or anal intercourse or through oral sex. It can also be passed without intercourse, through genital-to-genital contact with an infected person.

Herpes migrates from the point of contact on the skin down the nearest nerve to a ganglion (mass of nerve cells) near the base of the spine. The virus can lay dormant (inactive) in that ganglion for long periods of time. When it reactivates, it can travel through all the nerves that run out of the ganglion. It then surfaces on the skin and mucous membranes, where it produces blisters and lesions. These can occur on the genitals, buttocks, groin, and the upper thighs.

Genital herpes can be transmitted from an infected mother to her baby as the baby passes through the birth canal during delivery. A woman who is infected before she becomes pregnant has antibodies in her bloodstream. These antibodies are proteins produced by the immune system to fight off infection. The antibodies pass to the unborn baby and give the child some protection from catching herpes at birth. The greatest risk to the unborn child comes if the mother contracts herpes late in her pregnancy. Then the baby has a 50 percent chance of contracting herpes at birth.

For the first few weeks of a genital herpes infection, before the body has time to build up immunity to the virus, infected persons can sometimes spread the virus to other parts of their own body. This can happen by touching the infected area and then immediately touching another part of the body. This phenomenon is called autoinoculation and is uncommon. In persons with weakened immune systems (such as those with HIV/AIDS), the virus can spread throughout the body, a process called dissemination. This, too, is rare.

The herpes virus is quickly inactivated when it dries. For this reason, it is unlikely to be transmitted on dry towels, toilet seats, and other inanimate objects. Herpes cannot be caught in swimming pools or hot tubs unless someone has unprotected sex with an infected partner in one of those settings.

WHAT ARE THE SYMPTOMS OF GENITAL HERPES?

An estimated 20 percent of people who become infected with genital herpes never have symptoms and never know they are infected. Many of the remaining 80 percent, like Daniel, may not recognize their symptoms as genital herpes. All can pass their infection to others, however.

If symptoms develop, they usually first arise within two to twenty days of infection. Initial symptoms may be a bump or red area and itching, burning, or tingling of the skin. These first symptoms are termed the prodrome period. They can serve as a warning to a person with genital herpes that he or she is very infectious and is going to have an outbreak (an occurrence of herpes blisters).

Not every person with genital herpes experiences prodrome. Many go right into the syndrome period, when a variety of symptoms can occur. The most characteristic are blisters, usually about the size of a pinhead (although they can be larger), which appear alone or in clusters. These can arise on the genitals, buttocks, groin, anal area, and pubic hair region. They are often itchy and can also be very painful. Tiny slits or painful ulcers can form when blisters burst. Blisters and sores that occur on skin surfaces usually scab over as they heal. Those that occur on mucous membranes do not.

Other symptoms of a genital herpes infection can include:
- Fever, nausea, chills, muscle aches, tiredness, and headaches
- Difficulty and pain during urination

- Swollen, painful lymph nodes in the groin
- Weakness, pain, or tenderness in the lower back, legs, groin, and buttocks
- Numbness in the genital area or lower back

Symptoms of genital herpes normally last five to seven days but may last as long as six weeks. They may be so slight that infected persons never realize they are having an outbreak. On the other hand, they can be very painful and traumatic, causing infected people to miss work or school.

Many infected individuals mistake their herpes symptoms for something else. For instance, they may experience pain during urination and believe they have a bladder infection. Women may mistake vaginal discharge for a yeast infection. They may use antibiotics or over-the-counter yeast medications and think they have successfully treated their problem because the symptoms go away. In fact, the herpes infection has just subsided for a time and has the potential to recur later.

Women with genital herpes tend to experience more severe symptoms than men do. Persons with weakened immune systems generally have outbreaks that are longer and more severe as well. The primary episode of herpes is usually the most severe and takes longer to heal than later outbreaks.

In some cases, genital herpes infections can become serious. The virus can inflame the lining of the spinal cord, causing viral meningitis. Symptoms include stiff neck and sensitivity to light. Oral herpes infections can cause encephalitis—inflammation of the brain—with headache, fever, and seizures. Half of babies who are infected with herpes at birth die or suffer permanent neurological damage. Others can develop serious problems that affect the brain, eyes, or skin.

WILL I ALWAYS HAVE SYMPTOMS OF GENITAL HERPES?

Until experts find a cure or develop a vaccine for genital herpes, the virus remains an incurable infection. However, the first bout of symptoms normally disappears after about a week, and the virus can remain dormant for months at a time. Infected individuals feel perfectly healthy when they are symptom free. However, they will have periods of asymptomatic shedding (shedding without symptoms). Shedding is a condition in which the herpes virus is present on the skin and can be easily passed to others. Everyone who has genital herpes will shed at some point between outbreaks. A person cannot know when asymptomatic shedding is occurring, but experts find that people seem to shed most frequently just before and after outbreaks. During outbreaks, a person with herpes experiences symptomatic shedding (shedding with symptoms) and is very infectious.

One of the unpleasant characteristics of genital herpes is that it is recurrent—that is, outbreaks can occur repeatedly. Some people cynically call it "the disease that keeps on giving." Symptoms appear at random times, often at the most untimely moments such as before a big test, at the beginning of a new relationship, or at the start of a new job. Some people experience eight or more outbreaks a year. The average is four or five. Over time, outbreaks usually become less frequent.

WHAT TRIGGERS OUTBREAKS OF GENITAL HERPES?

Experts do not fully understand what causes the herpes virus to become active, but various factors seem to trigger outbreaks. These can include emotional and physical stress, fatigue, illness, and certain kinds of food such as nuts or chocolate. They might also be hormonal changes related to menstruation and pregnancy, poor eating habits, trauma to the skin, or exposure to sunlight. Although infected people can take preventive measures, sometimes outbreaks occur even when they do everything they can to avoid triggering the virus.

WHAT ABOUT THE EMOTIONAL SIDE EFFECTS OF GENITAL HERPES?

The emotional and psychological ramifications of genital herpes can be more distressing than its physical symptoms. Many people are deeply disturbed to learn that they have an incurable, contagious disease that can recur at any time. They feel anxious and guilty, knowing that they can infect future sexual partners despite all precautions. They are afraid that they will be rejected when they tell a new partner about their infection. One study by the American Social Health Association (ASHA), an authority on STDs, found that more than 60 percent of people rate genital herpes as being very traumatic, second only to HIV/AIDS.

Common emotional reactions to genital herpes can include anger, depression, isolation, and shame. Some people avoid sexual relationships for a long time, especially if they have once been rejected because of their infection. Some people decide to limit their sexual relationships to other people who have herpes too. Some people elect not to tell—a choice that often backfires when a sexual partner breaks out with herpes and demands to know where the infection came from.

Proper counseling and medical treatment can make genital herpes a manageable condition. Learning how to tell others of a sexually transmitted infection, learning to cope with genital herpes outbreaks, and learning how to lower the risk of infecting future sexual partners can help build confidence. These skills will also enable a person to successfully manage a genital herpes infection over the course of a lifetime.

HOW DOES A DOCTOR DIAGNOSE GENITAL HERPES?

Anyone who thinks he or she might have genital herpes should be tested as soon as possible. A delay in being tested can make an accurate diagnosis more difficult and increases the risk that others will be infected. Persons who suspect they are infected should stop having sex, especially unprotected sex, until they know how to limit the risk of infecting others.

Several tests are available for genital herpes, and all must be performed by a doctor or another health-care expert. The most common and reliable is the lesion culture test in which the doctor takes a swab or scraping of blisters or lesions and sends it to a laboratory to be analyzed. Antigen detection tests, performed on material taken from blisters, are also reliable. A positive result means that the genital herpes virus is present. A negative result may mean that no infection exists. It can also mean that there was no virus in that particular lesion. When test results are negative but symptoms of herpes are present, a follow-up test should be performed. Both culture and antigen detection tests must be performed while a person is having an outbreak.

Diagnosing genital herpes when a person is not having an outbreak involves blood tests and laboratory analysis and has long presented problems for doctors. The ELISA test and the Western blot immunoassay test both look for antibodies to the virus in the blood. However, the ELISA test does not distinguish between HSV-1 and HSV-2 infections, so patients who test positive cannot know whether they have oral or genital herpes. The Western blot test is highly accurate in its results but is expensive and not widely available.

Several less expensive tests promise to make diagnosis of genital herpes much easier in the future. The Food and Drug Administration (FDA) has approved at least two procedures that rely on analyzing infected blood. Both are proving to be reliable, rapid, and capable of distinguishing between HSV-1 and 2.

WHAT IS THE TREATMENT FOR GENITAL HERPES?

Treatment for genital herpes is designed to reduce pain and discomfort, shorten the length of outbreaks, and suppress their recurrence. This is usually done in two ways: with drug therapy and through alternatives to traditional medical care. A doctor should always be consulted to determine the best combination and course of treatment.

DRUG THERAPY

In recent years, several prescription antiviral drugs have been proven to shorten the length of outbreaks of genital herpes. These include acyclovir, valacyclovir, and famciclovir. Such medications do not prevent infection or kill the virus. They prevent the virus from replicating (reproducing).

Antiviral drugs need to be started within seventy-two hours of the beginning of an outbreak to be most effective. They must be taken for ten days. If babies who are born with genital herpes are treated immediately after birth with acyclovir, their chances of avoiding the effects of the disease are greatly increased.

During the first year of infection, when outbreaks may be most frequent and severe, antiviral medications can be taken at a slightly lower dosage and for an indefinite length of time to suppress (lessen) flare-ups. If taken suppressively, medication can reduce the number of outbreaks in 80 percent of people and eliminate symptoms completely in 50 percent.

Infected people can take several steps to ensure that maximum relief is obtained from prescribed medications. They include:

- Keeping blisters and lesions dry to speed healing
- Wearing loose clothing for comfort
- Being tested for other health conditions that may be weakening the immune system
- Trying a different antiviral medication if the one being used is not providing satisfactory relief
- Making sure the dosage of medicine is correct (check with your doctor)
- Identifying triggers that may bring on an outbreak—stress, fatigue, certain foods, etc.—and avoiding them if possible

ALTERNATIVE TREATMENTS

Many people with genital herpes claim that alternative approaches to controlling herpes work as well as or better than antiviral medication. However, some alternative remedies are expensive, some have not been proven safe, and many are not effective for most people. The following, used with antiviral medications, may be beneficial. You may want to consult with your medical doctor before pursuing any of these approaches.

Stress reduction techniques. Stress may bring on an outbreak of genital herpes, although there is no scientific proof of this. Outbreaks can certainly increase stress and make coping with symptoms more difficult, however. One or more of the following can reduce stress, improve the sense of well-being, and help with other emotional aspects of living with herpes: counseling, regular exercise, relaxation exercises, meditation, biofeedback, or participation in support groups for people with genital herpes.

Acupuncture. Acupuncture is the ancient Chinese practice of inserting small needles at certain key points on the human body to relieve a variety of conditions. Some people with genital herpes maintain that this therapy decreases the pain associated with outbreaks. There are no scientific studies to prove that acupuncture reduces the frequency of genital herpes outbreaks, however.

Nutrition and supplements. Experts have proved that a nutritious diet helps support a strong immune system, which can help lessen outbreaks of genital herpes. Some people believe that taking vitamin C, vitamin E, and zinc may boost the immune system. People with genital herpes who determine that certain foods trigger herpes outbreaks should avoid those foods.

Tea. Many people have found that damp black or green tea bags, placed on herpes sores, can be soothing. Some people believe that drinking green tea can inhibit the virus. Soaking in a warm bath in which several tea bags have been steeped can be both relaxing and pain reducing for people with genital herpes.

Drying agents. Substances such as cornstarch and rubbing alcohol, which dry out the skin, may promote healing of herpes lesions. Alcohol will sting when applied, however.

Ice. Cold compresses or ice, wrapped in a thin towel and applied directly to blisters or lesions, may lessen the severity of symptoms. Some people believe that ice may prevent an outbreak if it is applied during the prodromal warning period.

Some people believe drinking green tea can prevent outbreaks of genital herpes.

CHAPTER FIVE

WHAT YOU SHOULD KNOW
ABOUT HIV/AIDS

N*athan knew that he had contracted HIV in one of two ways. He had been infected either from having unprotected sex with many partners, both men and women, or from sharing infected needles while doing drugs. When he was released from the hospital, he went back to the streets, but his attitude was changing. Nathan no longer felt invincible. And knowing he posed a risk of infection to others, he stopped working as a prostitute.*

Then, within one week, two of Nathan's friends died of drug overdoses. Shaken up, Nathan decided to return home. Nathan's parents welcomed him back, although they still disagreed on many issues. They managed to overlook their differences, however. Last fall, Nathan enrolled in community college and began working to earn his general equivalency diploma.

Nathan still feels healthy, although he is on a heavy regimen of pills and sees the doctor regularly. Knowing of the many advances in AIDS treatment, Nathan takes a positive attitude. He even expects to live long enough to see a cure for the disease.

WHAT IS HIV/AIDS?

AIDS is the most complex of all STDs. It is caused by HIV, a retrovirus that destroys the immune system. The function of the body's immune system is to fight disease. Its failure leaves a person open to infection and illness. Retroviruses are a family of viruses characterized by a unique mode of replication (reproduction) in which ribonucleic acid (RNA) plays a key role. (RNA is a nucleic acid associated with the control of cellular chemical activity.)

The immune system fights disease in several ways. It produces white blood cells, known as lymphocytes, some of which engulf and destroy worn-out cells, cancer cells, and disease-causing agents (pathogens) such as bacteria, fungi, and viruses. Some lymphocytes react to invading foreign bodies by forming antibodies,

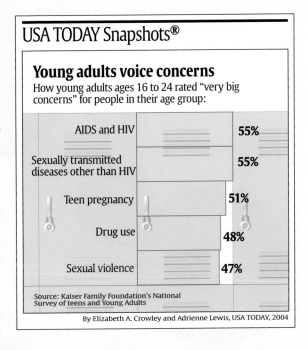

USA TODAY Snapshots®

Young adults voice concerns

How young adults ages 16 to 24 rated "very big concerns" for people in their age group:

AIDS and HIV	55%
Sexually transmitted diseases other than HIV	55%
Teen pregnancy	51%
Drug use	48%
Sexual violence	47%

Source: Kaiser Family Foundation's National Survey of teens and Young Adults

By Elizabeth A. Crowley and Adrienne Lewis, USA TODAY, 2004

which attach to the invaders, inactivate them, and mark them for destruction.

When HIV invades the body, it targets two other types of lymphocytes, the T-helper and T-suppressor cells, which regulate the immune system by controlling the strength and quality of all immune responses. HIV inserts its genetic material (the viral RNA) into the T cells, replicates inside the cells, and eventually destroys the cells as it goes on to infect others. When HIV first infects the body, a large amount of virus circulates in the system and the number of T cells goes down.

The body's immune system is usually strong enough to suppress the virus for a time. At some point, however, the virus gains the upper hand and the numbers of T cells start dropping significantly. It is then that a person's immunity becomes seriously impaired.

HIV Replication

1. An HIV particle meets a T cell. The knobby protein key on HIV's outer coat fits snugly into the T cell's receptor site. Attachment begins.

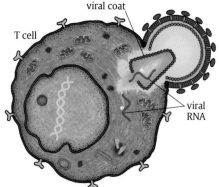

2. HIV's outer coat fuses with the outside membrane of the T cell.

3. Once inside the T cell, the virus sheds its coat. Two strands of RNA are released into the T cell.

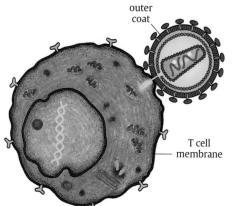

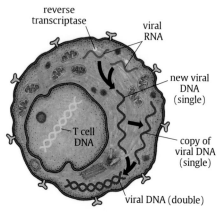

4. Reverse transcriptase converts a single strand of DNA from the two strands of viral RNA. Ribonuclease chops off the old RNA from the DNA copy. Then polymerase makes another exact copy of the new viral DNA and links the strands of DNA.

5. The brand-new double strand of viral DNA moves into the nucleus of the T cell. Once inside, integrase fuses the viral DNA with the T cell's DNA. Hijacking is complete.

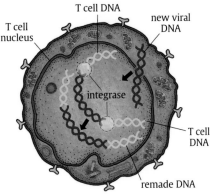

T cell DNA

new viral DNA

T cell nucleus

integrase

T cell DNA

remade DNA

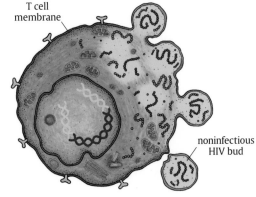

T cell membrane

proteins

mRNA

remade DNA

T cell nuceus

transcriptase

6. The remade DNA begins issuing orders for the production of proteins necessary to build new HIV particles. Using instructions in the form of messenger RNA and transfer RNA, ribosomes in the T cell begin assembling amino acids into large, inactive proteins. These proteins move to the cell membrane.

7. At the membrane, the HIV particles are released from the T cell by a process called budding. The young HIV particles are not infectious.

T cell membrane

noninfectious HIV bud

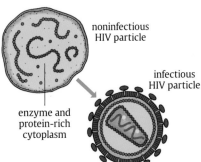

noninfectious HIV particle

infectious HIV particle

enzyme and protein-rich cytoplasm

8. Protease molecules split the large proteins inside the HIV particle into a bunch of smaller proteins and enzymes. With that, the HIV particle is a mature, infectious retrovirus.

The person is then considered to have AIDS and is at high risk of developing a variety of opportunistic infections (OIs) and diseases that can prove fatal.

At the end of 2010, the CDC estimated that more than one million people were infected with HIV in the United States. From the beginning of the epidemic in 1981 through 2007, more

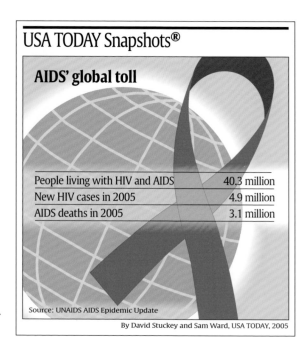

USA TODAY Snapshots®

AIDS' global toll

People living with HIV and AIDS	40.3 million
New HIV cases in 2005	4.9 million
AIDS deaths in 2005	3.1 million

Source: UNAIDS AIDS Epidemic Update

By David Stuckey and Sam Ward, USA TODAY, 2005

than 576,000 Americans have died of AIDS. With the improvement in scientific understanding of HIV/AIDS—along with better drugs to control the virus—HIV/AIDS has become a more manageable disease in the United States than when it first appeared. As a result, fewer Americans are dying each year from the OIs that were once a death sentence for people with HIV/AIDS.

At first, HIV/AIDS was predominantly a disease of gay men and hemophiliacs. (Hemophilia is a condition in which the body cannot effectively stop bleeding. To replace lost blood, hemophiliacs often require blood transfusions. Before blood supplies were routinely tested for HIV, hemophiliacs who received infected blood could become infected with the disease.) But over time, a rapid rise in infection rates was seen in heterosexuals who shared drug injection paraphernalia. There was also a rapid rise in infection rates in heterosexual women who had been infected by their sexual partners. In the twenty-first century, women and teenagers are two growing at-risk groups.

The HIV virus passes through breaks in the skin. For this reason, people who are infected with STDs that cause sores or rashes are at greater risk for contracting HIV than those who do not have these types of STDs.

HOW IS HIV TRANSMITTED?

HIV can be spread in three ways—sexual transmission, contact with infected blood, and transmission from mother to child. Sexual transmission includes unprotected vaginal or anal intercourse, oral-genital sex, or other genital contact where semen or vaginal fluids are passed between sexual partners. The risk of becoming infected after one instance of anal or genital contact is somewhere between one in ten and one in three hundred, depending on the virus level in the infected partner's system.

Transmission by contact with infected blood can take place in the following ways:

- Transfusions in which a person receives infected blood or blood product. In the twenty-first century, the risk of infection from blood is very low in the United States, since supplies are carefully screened for HIV.
- A stick with a needle that has infected blood on it. Health-care workers are at risk for infection in this manner. Their risk of infection depends on how much virus is on the needle and on how recently the needle was used. HIV cannot be transmitted through blood that has dried out in a syringe. However, although blood dries quickly when exposed to air, it may take days or even weeks for the blood in a syringe to dry. Still, health-care workers in the United States follow strict precautions for the disposal of

USA TODAY
HEALTH REPORTS:
DISEASES AND DISORDERS

www.usatoday.com

USA TODAY
Life
SECTION D

July 13, 2010

From the Pages of USA TODAY

National strategy on AIDS focuses on new infections, testing

President Obama gathered AIDS experts at the White House today to launch the first national strategy designed to cut new infections, boost the number of people who get tested and treated, and reduce disparities in access to care. The report notes that 1.1 million people in the USA are living with HIV, the virus that causes AIDS, and an additional 56,000 become infected each year, according to statistics from the U.S. Centers for Disease Control and Prevention.

Yet many Americans no longer view HIV as an urgent health problem, despite the misery it causes and its potential for further spread, the report says. "Unless we take bold actions," it warns, "we face a new era of rising infections, greater challenges in serving people living with HIV, and higher health care costs."

These actions include intensifying HIV prevention efforts in communities hit hard-

syringes, and don't reuse them. They are at a very low risk of becoming infected with HIV.

- Reuse of dirty needles or other infected paraphernalia related to intravenous drug use. (Intravenous drugs are injected into the bloodstream through needles.) Persons who use intravenous drugs such as heroin and methamphetamines and who share needles run a high risk of becoming infected with HIV.

- Contamination with infected blood on mucous membranes or through a break in the skin. Such contamination could possibly occur through French (open-mouth) kissing or through sharing razors or toothbrushes because of the possibility of contact with blood or open sores. The risk depends on how much virus is est by the disease; the use of a variety of prevention methods because "no single 'magic bullet' will stem the tide of new HIV infections"; and the first national effort in decades to educate "all Americans about the threat of HIV and how to prevent it."

By 2015, the White House seeks to:
• Reduce new HIV infections by 25%.
• Cut the rate of the virus' spread by 30%, from five people a year infected per every 100 living with HIV to 3.5 per 100.
• Increase from 79% to 90% the percentage of HIV-positive people who know they're infected with the virus so they can get treatment.

Michael Saag of the University of Alabama-Birmingham, president of the HIV Medical Association, praises the effort to reduce new infections as "obtainable and pretty realistic." Judy Auerbach, director of the San Francisco AIDS Foundation, one of a group of activists that pushed Obama and other presidential candidates for a national strategy during the last election, says the report "reflects the sense that we need to hone in on a few key things that must be done to really radically reduce infections and the size of the epidemic in the U.S." Auerbach says the line between prevention and treatment "has become blurred" because research shows that people who know they're HIV-positive and get treated are less likely to spread HIV. That's partly because people who know they're infected are more cautious with sexual partners. Evidence also suggests that people who get treated are less infectious even if they do engage in unsafe sex.

—*Steve Sternberg*

present and the size of the break in the skin. In most cases, the risk appears to be extremely low.

Transmission from mother to fetus during pregnancy and from mother to baby during childbirth or breastfeeding are additional means by which HIV can be spread. A baby born to an HIV-positive mother has at least a 12 to 13 percent chance of being infected at birth. The risk is about 30 percent if the mother is newly infected or has full-blown AIDS. Drug therapy given to an infected mother during pregnancy can significantly decrease a baby's chance of becoming infected. HIV testing of pregnant women is not mandatory, so infected pregnant women may not know they are infected.

HIV does not seem to be transmitted in the following ways:
- Sneezing, coughing, or breathing on food
- Casual contact such as hugging, shaking hands, using public toilets, touching doorknobs, or sharing drinking fountains
- Contact with urine, feces, sputum, sweat, or nasal secretions (unless blood is clearly visible)
- Insect or animal bites
- Sharing work or home environments

WHAT ARE THE SYMPTOMS OF HIV AND AIDS?

HIV often does not produce symptoms immediately after infection, although a newly infected person is highly contagious. If symptoms do occur, they can be mistaken for flu. They can include sore throat, fatigue, fever, headache and muscle aches, nausea and lack of appetite, swollen glands, and a rash over the entire body. Symptoms disappear after one to four weeks, and a person may not realize that he or she has been infected with HIV.

A period without symptoms follows initial HIV infection. This period may last up to ten years. Individuals are not as infectious during this time as they are in the beginning or when AIDS develops. All the same, people who know they are infected are still contagious and should make decisions accordingly.

Over time, as the body's immune system weakens, symptoms reappear and eventually worsen. These symptoms include fatigue, shortness of breath, general discomfort, night sweats, persistent fever, swollen lymph nodes, diarrhea, and unexplained weight loss. Unlike earlier symptoms, these are usually severe enough that an individual will seek treatment. The body's weakened immune system also allows a variety of mild infections such as thrush (a fungal mouth infection) and vaginal yeast infections to develop. At this stage, infected persons are very contagious due to high levels of virus in the blood.

As the immune system fails, the body's T cell count drops. When a person's helper T cell count is 200 or lower, that person is considered to have AIDS. As AIDS progresses, infected individuals get sick with various opportunistic infections. These are conditions that normally are not life threatening but that can become deadly when a person has low immunity. These OIs can include *Pneumocystis carinii* pneumonia, toxoplasmosis (a parasitic infection), tuberculosis, severe herpes infections, fungal infections, Kaposi's sarcoma (a rare, aggressive form of cancer), and non-Hodgkin's lymphoma (cancer of the lymph system). Women with AIDS have a higher occurrence of cervical cancer than do uninfected women. They are also more likely than men to have oral fungal infections; bacterial pneumonia infections; and progressive multifocal leukencephalopathy (PML), a viral infection of the central nervous system.

As AIDS progresses, illnesses become more frequent and more severe. Eventually, untreated people with AIDS are unable to recover from the many illnesses that attack the body. They become thin, weak, and cannot perform the functions of everyday life. Death from the OIs related to AIDS is often a slow, painful, and traumatic experience both for those with the disease and for those who love and care for them.

Children who are infected with HIV generally develop AIDS much more quickly than do adults, and the progress of their disease tends to be more rapid. Symptoms of AIDS in children include most of those in adults. However, children also suffer from more bacterial, viral, and fungal infections than do adults. HIV infection can slow the growth of children and impair their intellectual development and coordination as well.

WHAT SHOULD I KNOW BEFORE GETTING TESTED FOR HIV

Deciding to be tested for HIV infection can be difficult. So can receiving a positive diagnosis. Some teens ask a family member or close friend to come to the appointment for support. Some people also find it helpful to work with a counselor if the diagnosis is positive for HIV.

Testing for HIV/AIDS can be done confidentially and anonymously. Most HIV testing centers offer either confidential or anonymous testing. Testing could be provided at clinics, doctor's offices, hospitals, or state health departments. Normally, medical procedures carried out by a doctor or a clinic are confidential. This means they are part of a person's medical record and can be released only with his or her written permission.

Some teens don't want their parents to know that they're being tested for HIV/AIDS. But parents have access to the teen's medical records. In this situation, the teen could choose to take an anonymous diagnostic test that allows them to identify themselves only by a first name or a number. With an anonymous test, only the patient receives the results of the procedure. An anonymous test can be performed as an in-clinic procedure or with an at-home kit. Only an FDA-approved HIV home sample collection kit should be used for this purpose. There is only one FDA-approved kit, manufactured by Home Access Health Corporation. The kit can be purchased on the Internet. Numerous other kits, which are widely advertised, should be avoided.

HOW DOES A DOCTOR DIAGNOSE HIV/AIDS?

Diagnosing HIV. Medical professionals test for and diagnose HIV infection by looking for the presence of specific antibodies in the blood or saliva using the ELISA test. Because it takes time for antibodies to be produced by the body, however, a reliable diagnosis cannot be made until three months after possible infection. To confirm a positive ELISA test, medical professionals look for antibodies by using the Western blot immunoassay test. Both tests are highly accurate, and when used in combination, they identify most cases of HIV infection.

The p24 antigen test detects early infection more quickly than antibody tests do. It is often used by blood banks to screen out infected blood. This test is also used to detect infection in babies born to HIV-infected mothers. All such babies are born with HIV antibodies circulating in their blood. For this reason, they will automatically test positive to the ELISA and the Western blot immunoassay tests whether or not they are actually infected.

Diagnosing AIDS. Doctors consider HIV to have progressed into AIDS if a person's T-helper cell count has fallen below 200 cells per cubic millimeter of blood. (The normal level of T-helper cells in the blood is about 1,000 per cubic millimeter.) The presence of at least one of twenty-seven indicator infections such as *Pneumocystis carinii* pneumonia, toxoplasmosis, pulmonary tuberculosis, or invasive cervical cancer can also be grounds for a positive diagnosis of AIDS if there is no other reason for immune system damage.

The viral load, a measurement of how much virus is in the blood, is also used to track the progression of HIV to AIDS. A patient with a high viral load has more than 100,000 HIV particles per cubic millimeter of blood. This means the patient's immune system is at risk, leaving that person open to opportunistic infections. If a person has fewer than 10,000 virus particles per cubic millimeter of blood then the viral load will be undetectable. An undetectable viral load does not mean the patient has no HIV in his or her blood. It does, however, show that the patient's immune system is still working effectively.

WHAT IS THE TREATMENT FOR HIV/AIDS?

Although there is still no cure for HIV/AIDS, doctors are questioning whether a cutting-edge medical treatment in Germany may have cured one person. Known as the Berlin patient, he received a bone marrow transplant in 2007 as a treatment for leukemia. The donor for this transplant has an unusual genetic mutation that makes him immune to nearly all strains of HIV. Since the transplant, doctors have not been able to detect HIV in the Berlin patient. Such a transplant, a highly risky procedure, would be unthinkable as a regular cure for HIV/AIDS. It is hoped, however, that this medical breakthrough may help lead to a cure.

Researchers have made many promising and successful developments in the treatment of HIV/AIDS since the 1980s, when the disease was first identified. In developed countries such as the United States, drug therapy, counseling, and alternatives to traditional medicine allow people with HIV/AIDS to manage the disease much as they would a chronic illness. However, the expensive drugs used to treat HIV/AIDS and the funding to pay for those treatments are not always readily available in developing nations. For those without access to these treatments, the disease is still usually fatal.

DRUG THERAPY

Management of HIV and AIDS is a complicated process and involves many visits to the doctor or health-care facility. Individual medication plans must be set up and managed. Regular blood tests are necessary to monitor levels of T-helper cells and viral load levels and to see if medications are effectively suppressing the virus. Opportunistic infections must be treated and controlled to lower the risk of fatal complications. Because of such complexities, treatment is usually ongoing.

Despite the difficulties, advances in pharmaceutical research have brought powerful new drugs to treat HIV/AIDS. There are no drugs currently available that kill HIV. However, a combination of antiretroviral drugs (ARVs) is prescribed as part of the highly active antiretroviral therapy (HAART) treatment. An antiretroviral drug is used to treat infections caused by retroviruses, such as HIV. HAART is effective in inhibiting the progression of HIV to AIDS, thereby prolonging the life and health of an infected person.

The first ARVs to be developed in the late 1980s and early 1990s were nucleoside reverse transcriptase inhibitors (NRTIs). These were followed by non-nucleoside reverse transcriptase inhibitors (NNRTIs). Both drugs, which are still used, work to block the conversion of HIV genetic material from ribonucleic acid to deoxyribonucleic acid (DNA). Protease inhibitors, first approved in 1995, are the most powerful of the ARVs. They can slow the disease by interrupting the release and function of new viral cells, rendering HIV particles noninfectious.

Some other ARVs are fusion inhibitors and integrase inhibitors, which are effective in fighting drug-resistant strains of HIV. Chemokine coreceptor inhibitors prevent HIV from attaching to and then entering the target cell.

Experts have found that combination therapy works best in treating HIV. When two or three drugs are combined, HIV levels in the blood can be reduced to almost undetectable levels. For those just beginning ARV therapy, a combination of two drugs is usually prescribed. Daily doses of medication can total up to twenty pills, however, and side effects are often severe. It can also be difficult to remember to take all medications correctly. Failure to follow instructions can be disastrous because only a few mistakes can allow HIV to become resistant to drug treatment.

To get the best results from drug therapy, persons with HIV/AIDS are encouraged to adopt as healthy a lifestyle as possible.

www.usatoday.com

USA TODAY

News
SECTION A

November 24, 2010

From the Pages of USA TODAY

HIV drug, drop in new cases give hope for prevention

The global AIDS epidemic has taken a turn for the better with fewer new infections than a decade ago, but overall progress is slow and much work lies ahead, the United Nations' leading AIDS agency reported Tuesday.

A new report by UNAIDS says that 2.6 million people became infected with HIV, the AIDS virus, in 2009, about 20% fewer new infections than 1999 when the epidemic was at its peak. The news comes a day after researchers reported that a daily dose of a widely available HIV drug, Truvada, can prevent infections in gay and bisexual men.

Greater access to treatment has also driven down AIDS deaths and increased the number of people living with HIV. Deaths dropped from 2.1 million worldwide in 2004 to 1.8 million last year, a drop of nearly 20%. By the end of last year, 33.3 million people were estimated to be living with an HIV infection, up from 32.8 million a year earlier.

"The decline in HIV infections globally is encouraging news," says Kevin Fenton, director of HIV prevention for the Centers for Disease Control and Prevention. "But real challenges lie ahead. For example, the 5 million people on treatment today represents only a third of the people in need."

"The reality is, because there's no cure, there's no vaccine, the only way to end the epidemic is by ending new infections,"

This includes eliminating smoking, drug use, and excessive alcohol consumption. It also includes regular exercise and a healthy diet. Patients are also encouraged to follow recommendations to protect themselves against other STDs and to protect others from catching HIV. They are instructed to be checked for tuberculosis regularly. HIV-infected women are also urged to have a Pap smear every six

Fenton says, adding "that's going to take a global push to adopt new approaches to prevention, expand HIV counseling and testing, and combat the stigma and discrimination that breeds risky behavior and keeps people from seeking preventive services and treatment."

Researchers say the Truvada drug could prove to be a key factor in the battle against HIV. A major study showed for the first time that Truvada, a drug duo widely used to treat the AIDS virus, can block HIV infection.

The drug duo consists of tenofovir and emtricitabine, packaged as a once-daily pill and sold in drugstores. It reduced HIV infections by an average of 44% among gay and bisexual men who took the drug, compared with those taking a placebo. Men who reported being the most diligent about taking their pill each day reaped an even bigger benefit, reducing their risk by 73%.

"This is a huge step forward," says lead researcher Robert Grant, at the J. David Gladstone Institutes at the University of California-San Francisco, a non-profit research foundation that carried out the study.

David Paltiel of Yale University [in Connecticut] says that his research shows that Truvada could be as cost-effective a prevention method as those used to combat heart disease, diabetes and cancer, despite its $8,700 annual cost.

The findings have bred new enthusiasm in a field where, for years, optimism was rare. Over 30 years, HIV has infected 40 million people. But this year alone, researchers have demonstrated that a pill and a vaginal gel (containing a component of Truvada) can prevent HIV and shown that a vaccine could work.

"This is a very exciting, dynamic time in HIV prevention research," said Alan Bernstein, head of the Global HIV Vaccine Enterprise, a non-profit effort to accelerate vaccine research. "It couldn't come at a better time. There's clearly a growing realization that we're not going to be able to treat our way out of this epidemic."

Over the next two or three years, researchers hope to determine whether Truvada also works in heterosexuals and drug users.

—Steve Sternberg

months to test for cervical cancer. A Pap smear is a test to detect cancerous or precancerous cells of the cervix.

COUNSELING

Emotional support is a vital part of HIV/AIDS treatment. A diagnosis of HIV/AIDS can be very traumatic. Guidance and counseling from a psychologist, social worker, or health-care worker can make a huge difference in dealing with emotional distress, in maintaining a sense of hope and purpose, and in continuing to live a healthy and productive life.

A variety of traditional and online self-help, support, stress management, and grief management communities are available to infected individuals. These communities can help make it possible to cope with the variety of feelings and social experiences that can be a part of living with HIV/AIDS. Counseling centers and churches also provide support and individual or group counseling. Family counseling can help parents or siblings of a person with HIV/AIDS deal with their responses to the disease. The Resources section at the end of this book shows where to find support organizations in your region or support communities online.

ALTERNATIVE TREATMENTS

Many people who have HIV/AIDS choose to combine traditional drug treatment and counseling with alternative treatments. These alternatives can include herbal therapy, acupuncture, massage, vitamins, and changes in diet. Practitioners of alternative forms of medicine can provide advice and guidance, either in person or through online sites. Before beginning such treatments, a person with HIV/AIDS should consult with a physician to ensure that no harmful effects will result from alternative medicines. Alternative therapies should supplement, not take the place of, drug therapy for HIV/AIDS treatment.

WHAT IS THE COST OF TREATMENT?

The cost of treatment for AIDS can be extremely high. After a number of years of treatment, totals can grow unmanageably large. People in developing countries are often unable to afford the most effective therapies that are available. This has changed for many people, however, as generic (not brand-name) ARVs become available. The generic drugs are much more affordable. This competition also forces brand-name pharmaceutical companies to slash their prices to compete. In the United States, government programs such the AIDS Drug Assistance Programs (ADAP) help pay for costly medications for those who have limited finances or do not have private insurance.

The ADAPs are state-run programs funded by federal grants. They are the primary source of expensive FDA-approved prescription drugs for those who can't afford them. The state ADAP programs were first funded in 1987 with the goal of making the powerful new antiretroviral drug AZT (azidothymidine) more widely available. They were officially written into law in 1990 and renewed and strengthened in 2006.

In addition to the ADAPs, various nonprofit organizations also assist those with HIV/AIDS who can't afford treatments. The ADAPs focus on providing drugs and do not focus on other needs. Nutritional support and other needs are met by groups such as the AIDS Assistance Program. This group receives no federal or state funding yet provides individuals with one hundred dollars per month in food vouchers to help improve their quality of life.

It is important to know of these financial-assistance options. But financial questions are not foremost in the minds of most teens when they think of AIDS. Because HIV/AIDS has become a more manageable disease, many Americans have become less careful about reducing their risk of contracting the disease. Despite medical advances, the most compelling concern for teens should still be that HIV is a killer—the top infectious disease in the world. The risk of infection is still very real, and teens should take effective precautions.

CHAPTER SIX

WHAT YOU SHOULD KNOW ABOUT GENITAL WARTS AND HEPATITIS B

For a while, Miguel thought about breaking up with Larissa. He was embarrassed by his genital warts, and he felt bad that he could infect her. Larissa was flatteringly eager to be with him, however. It seemed too hard to tell her about his condition. One weekend when her parents were away, she invited Miguel over to her home, and they went "all the way." Miguel offered to use a condom, but Larissa told him she was on the Pill, so he let the issue slide.

Now Miguel has an uncomfortable feeling that maybe he ought to have said something to Larissa about his infection. They have been sexually intimate for a month, and he still can't find the right words.

WHAT ARE GENITAL WARTS?

Despite Miguel's wishful thinking, if he continues to have unprotected sex with Larissa, she will probably catch genital warts (also known as venereal warts), one of the most common STDs in the United States. Genital warts are caused by the human papillomavirus (HPV), a family of more than seventy different types of viruses that cause warts on hands, feet, and genitals. Most people are infected with some type of HPV, although they may not have warts of any kind. About one-third of all types of human papillomavirus cause genital warts. The type of HPV that produces genital warts does not commonly cause warts on hands and feet and vice versa.

About one-half of all sexually active adults are infected with a type of HPV that causes genital warts, and the incidence of infection appears to be on the increase. An estimated six million new cases are diagnosed every year in the United States. The chances of getting

HPV through a sexual encounter with an infected person are high. About two-thirds of people who have repeated sexual contact with someone infected with genital warts will become infected within three months. The more partners a person has, the greater the chances of becoming infected with HPV.

Genital warts are very common among young people. Some studies show that one-third of all sexually active teens have genital HPV infections. Young women, particularly those who become sexually active before the age of eighteen, have a high risk of contracting genital HPV. This is because the cervix is not fully mature in the teen years and can be easily infected. The risk to men of all ages is significant as well. Between 60 and 90 percent of men whose partners are infected with genital warts also have HPV.

USA TODAY Snapshots®

Birth control pill turns 50 this year

Most popular birth control methods among U.S. women ages 15 to 44:

9% Vasectomy
18% Condoms
27% Tubal sterilization
31% Pill

Source: Alan Guttmacher Institute

By Anne R. Carey and Sam Ward, USA TODAY, 2010

According to some experts, smoking may increase a person's risk for developing genital warts because it suppresses the immune system, allowing HPV more chance to manifest itself. In one study of almost six hundred women, smokers were five times as likely to develop visible genital warts as were nonsmokers.

HOW IS HPV TRANSMITTED?

HPV lives in the skin and is transmitted through skin-to-skin contact during vaginal, anal, or oral-genital sex. HPV is not passed through blood, semen, or other body fluids. A person can be infectious even if no symptoms are present, but the risk is probably greatest if contact is made with the warts themselves. The thin mucous membranes of the vagina, vulva, penis, and scrotum are particularly prone to infection.

Babies can sometimes become infected with HPV at birth while passing through the birth canal of infected mothers. There is little or no risk of catching HPV from towels or other inanimate objects.

WHAT ARE THE SYMPTOMS OF HUMAN PAPILLOMAVIRUS?

Most people who are infected with the human papillomavirus have no symptoms at all. Visible symptoms are small bumps (warts), which usually develop between thirty to ninety days after initial infection. In a few people, warts may not appear until years after the initial infection.

With genital types of HPV, warts develop on the penis and scrotum, inside the urethra, around and inside the vagina, and on the cervix of the uterus. They may appear inside and around the anus, on the lower abdomen and upper thighs, and in the groin. Occasionally they occur in the mouth and throat or on the lips, eyelids, and nipples. A person may never know he or she has genital warts if this condition occurs only inside the urethra, on the walls of the vagina, or on the cervix.

Genital warts can look like regular warts. They may be flesh colored or darker, and they are usually harder than surrounding tissue. They may be flat or raised, single or multiple, large or small. They can grow and spread and assume a cauliflower-like appearance, or they may remain small and barely noticeable. They may itch, but they usually do not hurt unless they are scratched and become irritated.

Often genital warts go away without treatment. The virus does not disappear, however. It remains in the body indefinitely, and when it reactivates, new outbreaks of warts can occur. People can experience outbreaks of genital warts throughout their lifetime, although the virus commonly becomes less active as time passes.

WHAT ARE THE COMPLICATIONS OF HPV?

Most types of genital warts are harmless, but some can have dangerous consequences. Certain types of the HPV virus increase a person's chances of developing cancer in the genital area, particularly cancer of the penis, anus, vulva, and cervix.

According to the American Cancer Society, about 12,200 women develop cervical cancer every year, and about 4,200 of these women die from the disease. Certain types of HPV have been found to be responsible for cellular changes that can lead to cervical cancer. In fact, when cervical cancer lesions are examined under a microscope, HPV is detected about 100 percent

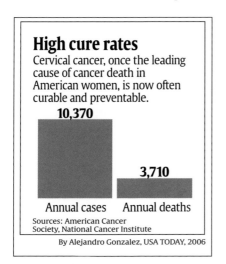

High cure rates

Cervical cancer, once the leading cause of cancer death in American women, is now often curable and preventable.

10,370 — Annual cases

3,710 — Annual deaths

Sources: American Cancer Society, National Cancer Institute

By Alejandro Gonzalez, USA TODAY, 2006

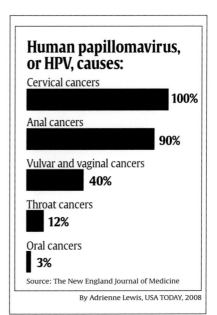

Human papillomavirus, or HPV, causes:

Cervical cancers — 100%

Anal cancers — 90%

Vulvar and vaginal cancers — 40%

Throat cancers — 12%

Oral cancers — 3%

Source: The New England Journal of Medicine

By Adrienne Lewis, USA TODAY, 2008

of the time. Women who have HPV, therefore, must be doubly sure to get a regular Pap smear every six months to detect early changes in the cervix that might indicate cervical cancer. The HPV DNA test, which can detect HPV on the cervix, is sometimes also used along with the Pap smear.

Genital warts not only increase the risk of cancer, but they can also cause problems during pregnancy, when they have a tendency to grow rapidly. If they enlarge, they can make urination difficult. If present on the wall of the vagina, they can cause obstruction during delivery of a baby. Infants born to infected mothers may develop warts on their larynx (voice box). This is a potentially life-threatening condition that requires frequent laser surgery to keep the baby's airways open.

HOW DOES A DOCTOR DIAGNOSE HUMAN PAPILLOMAVIRUS?

Human papillomavirus is almost always diagnosed by the presence of visible warts. Certain diagnostic techniques can detect the genetic material of the virus, but these are used to help to check patients for cervical cancer. They are not used as general tests for HPV.

People who suspect they may have genital warts need to be seen and diagnosed by an experienced health-care provider. The skin of the genitals is often naturally bumpy and irregular. A trained, professional eye may be necessary to decide what is normal and what is not. A procedure called a colposcopy is sometimes used to detect warts that may not otherwise be easily seen, such as those that grow on the cervix. A Pap smear can reveal abnormalities in cells consistent with HPV infection. However, the Pap smear is not a completely accurate diagnostic tool for HPV or other STDs. A person can have a normal Pap smear and still be infected with HPV or other STDs.

News
SECTION A

March 19, 2010

From the Pages of USA TODAY

HPV vaccine not reaching needy: Study says cervical cancer impacts poor states most

Acervical cancer vaccine is not getting to many of the girls who need it the most, a new study shows.

Mississippi and Arkansas, two of the nation's poorest states, also have the highest death rates from cervical cancer—a result of poor access to basic screenings and health care for a large number of women, says Peter Bach of New York's Memorial Sloan-Kettering Cancer Center.

Yet in Mississippi, where the vaccine could perhaps save the greatest number of lives, only 16% of teen girls in 2008 received the shot, called Gardasil, according to Bach's paper in Saturday's *The Lancet*. About 22% of Arkansas girls ages 13 to 17 got the vaccine, which costs $390 for three shots.

In the wealthier state of Rhode Island, where cervical cancer mortality is half as high as in Mississippi and Arkansas, 55% of girls received Gardasil, the paper says. Though there's nothing wrong with wealthier girls getting the vaccine, Bach says, the low vaccination rates in poor states are "a failure."

The Food and Drug Administration approved Gardasil in 2006 and another vaccine, Cervarix, in 2009. Both block infection with the cancer-causing human papillomavirus, or HPV.

Merck spokeswoman Pamela Eisele says the company has several programs to help poor women afford the shots.

Low-income girls also can get free vaccines from the federal Vaccines for Children program, says Lance Rodewald of the Centers for Disease Control and Prevention. Partly because of that program, 46% of girls in households with incomes below the poverty level received at least one HPV shot in 2008, compared with 36% of those above poverty level. The federal poverty level is $22,050 for a family of four, according to the Department of Health and Human Services.

But women's health activist Barbara Brenner of Breast Cancer Action says Bach's study highlights broad inequalities in American health care. "There are places in this country where women have nothing," Brenner says. "But we don't notice them until a story like this comes out."

—*Liz Szabo*

WHAT IS THE TREATMENT FOR GENITAL WARTS?

A cure for human papillomavirus is not yet known. Because most types of genital warts are not dangerous, some people choose to live with them and see if they go away on their own. In many cases, genital warts disappear without treatment. If warts are large, irritated and bleeding, or embarrassing, they can be removed.

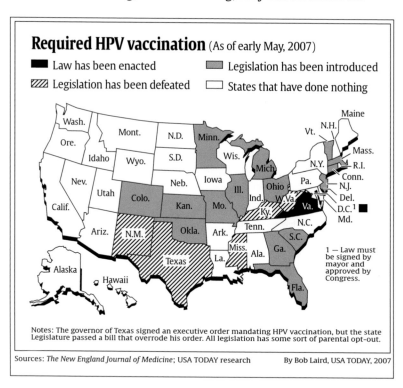

Required HPV vaccination (As of early May, 2007)

■ Law has been enacted   ▨ Legislation has been introduced
▨ Legislation has been defeated   □ States that have done nothing

1 — Law must be signed by mayor and approved by Congress.

Notes: The governor of Texas signed an executive order mandating HPV vaccination, but the state Legislature passed a bill that overrode his order. All legislation has some sort of parental opt-out.

Sources: *The New England Journal of Medicine*; USA TODAY research   By Bob Laird, USA TODAY, 2007

Medical professionals have several procedures for removal of genital warts. A doctor should be consulted to see which procedure is best, depending on the size, number, and location of the growths. Removal procedures include:

• Cryotherapy—freezing off warts with liquid nitrogen

- Physician-applied medications such as podophyllin and trichloracetic acid, or prescription medications such as imiquimod cream, applied directly to the surface of the warts
- Electrocautery (burning) or laser therapy
- Surgical removal
- Alpha interferon treatment—used when warts recur after removal by other means

All of these treatments can eliminate warts and may lower the risk of transmitting the virus to others. Removal does not guarantee that warts will not return, however. Most people who have genital warts removed will experience recurrences.

WHAT IS HEPATITIS B?

Hepatitis B is one of a family of hepatitis viruses. Unlike hepatitis A, which is spread through contaminated food and water, hepatitis B is commonly passed through an exchange of infected body fluids including blood, semen, vaginal secretions, fluid from wounds, and saliva. Hepatitis C is also a blood-borne strain that can cause severe liver damage and death, but it seems rarely to be passed through normal sexual contact. Other strains of the disease that are rare in the United States are hepatitis D (blood-borne) and E (commonly spread through contaminated drinking water).

Hepatitis B virus is a highly transmissible disease, about one hundred times more contagious than HIV. It can survive outside of the body for at least seven days on a dry surface. Although a vaccine is lowering the rate of infection, by 2008 about thirty-eight thousand Americans were infected annually, and about three thousand Americans die each year of complications from hepatitis B.

Those people at highest risk of catching hepatitis B are individuals who have unprotected sex with more than one partner, men who have sex with men, people who live with someone who has chronic hepatitis B, people who have jobs that involve contact with human blood, and people who travel to regions where hepatitis B is common. These regions include Southeast Asia, Africa, the Amazon Basin in South America, the Pacific Islands, and the Middle East. Teens whose parents were born in those regions are doubly at risk because a parent with chronic hepatitis B may pass the disease to them by nonsexual means. In the United States, the reported rate of new infections is highest in adults between the ages of twenty and forty-nine.

HOW IS HEPATITIS B TRANSMITTED?

Hepatitis B is commonly passed from person to person through unprotected sexual contact including vaginal, anal, and oral sex. Many people catch hepatitis B while sharing injectable drug paraphernalia with infected friends. Mothers can pass the virus to their unborn children during pregnancy and delivery. Unborn babies whose mothers are infected with hepatitis B have a greater than 80 percent chance of being born with hepatitis.

Other possible means of transmission include:

- Having regular household contact with an infected person through the sharing of toothbrushes, nail clippers, or razors (because of the risk of contact with blood or body fluids)
- Getting tattooed, having acupuncture treatment, or getting body parts pierced can be risky if unsterile needles are used. All these treatments generally occur in sterile environments. You should, however, ensure that the tattoo parlor, piercing parlor, or acupuncture clinic that you choose is a reputable, safe establishment.

- Receiving contaminated blood through a transfusion. The risk of this is rare in the United States because U.S. blood supplies have been routinely screened for hepatitis B since 1975 (and hepatitis C since 1990).
- Any other activity involving a transfer of infected body fluids through the skin, such as with a human bite.

WHAT ARE THE SYMPTOMS OF HEPATITIS B?

People infected with hepatitis B may have no symptoms, although they will still be infectious. About two-thirds of those with hepatitis B antibodies in their blood never recall having the disease.

For those who do show symptoms, these generally appear between one and four months after infection and can be mistaken for the flu. Symptoms then progress and can include:

- Achy joints
- Extreme tiredness and loss of appetite
- Mild fever
- Abdominal pain
- Diarrhea and light-colored bowel movements
- Nausea and vomiting
- Jaundice (yellowing of the skin and the whites of the eyes)
- Dark urine

Symptoms range from mild to severe and usually last about one to two months. A few patients experience liver failure and death shortly after infection. About 90 to 95 percent of people who are infected recover completely and then have lifelong immunity from becoming infected again. (They can, however, become infected with different strains of hepatitis.)

About 5 to 10 percent of infected individuals do not recover within

www.usatoday.com

USA TODAY

Life
SECTION D

January 23, 2006

From the Pages of USA TODAY

Hepatitis, 'the silent killer,' driven out of the shadows

There was a time when Arline Loh of Wilmington, Del., didn't tell people she has hepatitis B. "It carries such a stigma," says Loh, 57, an information technology expert who retired three months ago because of liver damage caused by the disease. "Hepatitis B is classified as an STD."

It can be transmitted sexually, but Loh contracted the disease at birth from her mother, who carried the virus. About 90% of babies who are infected at birth develop chronic infection, compared with 6% of those infected later in life. Until recent years, there was little the medical profession could do to help. Loh says the doctor who diagnosed her 17 years ago told her to "rest, and maybe you'll get better." That has changed. There are medications for hepatitis B. "Now, I don't want to be silent," Loh says. "Now there are drugs available to manage and treat this disease."

Hepatitis B can cause long-term, chronic infection that can lead to severe liver damage, cirrhosis or liver cancer. The diseases can go undetected for decades because they often cause no symptoms until serious liver damage has occurred.

Hepatitis B disproportionately affects Asians and Pacific Islanders, who account for over half of the more than 1.3 million carriers of the virus, says hepatitis researcher Samuel So, director of the Asian Liver Center at Stanford University School of Medicine [in California]. Hepatitis rates among Asian-Americans are higher because the rates are high in many of their countries of origin, according to the Asian Liver Center.

China, where Loh was born, bears the world's highest rate of hepatitis B, he says. About one in 10 are infected, and

six months and are considered chronically infected. (Babies who are born infected are at risk of becoming chronically infected as well.) About one million Americans are chronically infected with hepatitis B.

about half a million people there die each year. "We call it the silent killer," So says. "Many people who are infected don't know it because they feel perfectly healthy."

Studies show that 10% to 20% of Asian-Americans have chronic hepatitis B infection. And carriers with no symptoms can unwittingly pass it on to their sexual partners or to their children. Routine blood tests don't include the specific test to detect hepatitis B, he says, so patients should ask for it.

The hepatitis B vaccine is required for all newborns and adolescents who missed their baby shots. A hepatitis B vaccine also is recommended for adults, especially those in high-risk groups. Vaccination has helped reduce rates of hepatitis B from an average of 260,000 new cases a year in the 1980s, when the vaccine was licensed, to about 73,000 in 2003 [38,000 in 2008], according to the Centers for Disease Control and Prevention.

—Anita Manning

Arline Loh is working to promote awareness of hepatitis B. She holds some of the many medications she takes to treat her hepatitis and related illnesses.

One-third of people who are chronically infected go on to develop chronic active hepatitis, which can lead to serious damage of the liver (cirrhosis), liver cancer, and death. Two-thirds of those who are

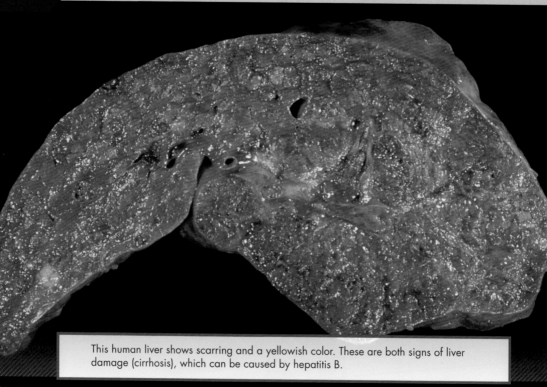

This human liver shows scarring and a yellowish color. These are both signs of liver damage (cirrhosis), which can be caused by hepatitis B.

chronically infected have chronic persistent hepatitis and suffer mild inflammation of the liver. They are still at some risk of developing cirrhosis and liver cancer, but their risk is not as great.

Chronically infected individuals are also carriers of the disease. This means they are contagious even though they show no outward symptoms of the virus. Although chronically infected individuals are commonly infected for the rest of their lives, they can and do spontaneously recover at times.

HOW DOES A DOCTOR DIAGNOSE HEPATITIS B?

Physical symptoms and abnormal liver function tests are the first clues to a doctor that a person may be infected with hepatitis. Specific blood tests that look for antibodies or virus antigens are necessary to confirm a diagnosis, however. In rare cases of chronic hepatitis, it may be necessary to perform a liver biopsy. This procedure involves examining a small sample of liver tissue under a microscope. A biopsy can determine the stage of infection and the extent of damage that has been done.

Anyone who is found to be infected with hepatitis B should also be tested for hepatitis D (delta hepatitis), a blood-borne strain that can also cause severe liver damage. Hepatitis D uses hepatitis B to reproduce and survive, and thus only infects people who have hepatitis B. Hepatitis D is transmitted through the sharing of infected needles and through sexual contact.

WHAT IS THE TREATMENT FOR HEPATITIS B?

There is no cure for hepatitis B, but in most cases, the infection goes away on its own. During the period when symptoms are present, doctors usually prescribe bed rest and plenty of fluids. Hospitalization is not necessary unless a person has other medical problems or is extremely ill.

People with chronic hepatitis infections sometimes benefit from treatment with injections of synthetic (produced artificially instead of by the body) interferon alfa-2b or peginterferon alfa-2a. Produced naturally by white blood cells, interferons are antiviral proteins that protect cells from infection by interfering with viral replication. The drug lamivudine is also used in some cases, but viral resistance to treatment may occur. Other antiviral drugs used to treat the disease are adefovir, entecavir, telbivudine, and tenofovir. Some patients have fewer or less severe side effects with one or another of these treatments.

People with liver failure as a result of hepatitis B can have their lives extended by a liver transplant. Because of the scarcity of available livers, however, only 200 to 250 hepatitis B patients are able to receive liver transplants each year. More than five thousand Americans die as the result of a chronic hepatitis B infection. For those who do receive a transplant, reinfection of the new liver is a possibility.

A VACCINE FOR HEPATITIS B

Hepatitis B may be incurable, but it is also totally preventable. A safe and effective vaccine—three shots over the course of six months—

A baby receives the hepatitis B vaccine. The CDC recommends that all babies be vaccinated for hepatitis B.

became available in 1982. The vaccine effectively eliminates the risk of infection for those who are properly immunized (receive the vaccine). Immunization against hepatitis B is also protection against hepatitis D.

The CDC recommends that all babies be vaccinated against hepatitis B at birth. Others who should be vaccinated include:

- Teens who have not been vaccinated, particularly teens who are sexually active or who practice tattooing or body piercing
- Teens whose parents come from Southeast Asia, Africa, the Amazon Basin in South America, the Pacific Islands, and the Middle East
- People who use intravenous drugs
- People such as nurses, doctors, dentists, laboratory workers, and paramedics, whose jobs expose them to human blood
- People who are partners of or live with someone with hepatitis B
- People who have multiple sexual partners
- Prison inmates
- People receiving dialysis (a treatment that cleanses the patient's blood after the kidneys have failed)

Anyone who is exposed to hepatitis B but who has not been immunized can get the vaccination series plus a dose of hepatitis B immunoglobulin, a collection of antibodies that boosts the immune system for a short time. The two together offer some protection against becoming infected. Children who are born to infected mothers stand a good chance of not becoming infected if they receive vaccinations plus immunoglobulin within twelve hours after birth.

CHAPTER SEVEN

HOW TO AVOID CATCHING AN STD

Celeste's STD infection is a thing of the past, but she still feels embarrassed every time she sees Kurtis at school. She wonders if the authorities notified him of his STD and if he knows that they found out because of her. Although she acted appropriately, Celeste still feels bad that she had to reveal that it was Kurtis who gave her gonorrhea.

Celeste has decided to learn from her mistake and be very careful not to mix alcohol and physical relationships in the future. She now realizes that anyone can get an STD, not just teens who are promiscuous or those who use drugs. To educate herself, Celeste did some online research on STDs, as well as checking out a book on the subject from her local library.

- Do you know you can eliminate your risk of catching an STD?
- Do you know that both regular condoms and female condoms greatly reduce your chances of contracting an STD?
- Do you know that birth control pills prevent pregnancy, but not STDs?
- Do you know that you should plan ahead so you can talk to your boyfriend or girlfriend about STDs before you decide to have sex?

STDs range from annoying, painful ailments to life-changing, life-threatening illnesses. Protecting yourself from them is more than just a good idea. It is an investment in a healthy future.

Many people in the United States choose to ignore STDs, however. They have sex with people they scarcely know and have sexual encounters while using alcohol and drugs. In studies of high school and college students, only about half of those who are sexually active use condoms every time they have sex, and nearly half report that they have had more than one sexual partner. Some teens say they have had seven or more partners.

Casual sex is risky business. Good schools, wealth, and good looks do not protect people from contracting STDs, which is a likely outcome of sexual contact with multiple partners or with people you don't know well. The pretty girl sitting across the aisle in math class could be infected with chlamydia, just as the boy next door might have genital herpes or HIV. Teens who tell themselves that taking a sexual risk just once is okay are making a big mistake. By making smart choices about sexual behavior, anyone can lower if not eliminate the risk of catching an STD.

ABSTINENCE—BE 100 PERCENT SURE

There is only one sure way to prevent catching an STD—total sexual abstinence. That means not engaging in vaginal, anal, or oral sex or any other sexual activity that involves genital contact with another person. It means no illegal intravenous drug use and sharing of needles.

Abstinence is not always a popular or easy choice to make. Some people believe that total abstention from sexual activity is impossible or even psychologically harmful for healthy, well-adjusted human beings. Such is not necessarily the case, however. Abstinence is practiced in many world religions, and some people still wait until marriage before having

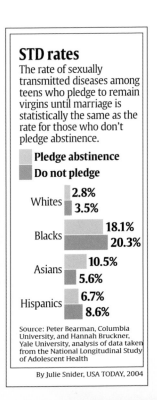

STD rates

The rate of sexually transmitted diseases among teens who pledge to remain virgins until marriage is statistically the same as the rate for those who don't pledge abstinence.

■ **Pledge abstinence**
■ **Do not pledge**

Whites
2.8%
3.5%

Blacks
18.1%
20.3%

Asians
10.5%
5.6%

Hispanics
6.7%
8.6%

Source: Peter Bearman, Columbia University, and Hannah Bruckner, Yale University, analysis of data taken from the National Longitudinal Study of Adolescent Health

By Julie Snider, USA TODAY, 2004

www.usatoday.com

News
SECTION A

July 30, 2007

From the Pages of USA TODAY

Abstinence-only fails to stop early pregnancies, diseases

After graduating from college, Sarah Audelo joined Teach for America and was assigned to the tiny Texas border town of La Joya. There, at Jimmy Carter High School, she noticed something odd. Despite the fact that her school enrolled only ninth- and tenth-graders, a noticeable number of girls were mothers caring for babies or pregnant. Midway through the school year, one of her 14-year-old students became pregnant.

Then, Audelo discovered that the school's sex education program only teaches abstinence. Teaching abstinence has always had a certain appeal. How many parents disagree with the notion that their teens should postpone sex? But abstinence-only programs aren't having much success.

That conclusion comes from an eight-year, government-funded study recently released by highly respected, non-partisan Mathematica Policy Research Inc. The study zeroed in on four programs, selected for their variety of approaches, and followed students for four to six years. The authors of the 164-page report didn't equivocate: There is no evidence that abstinence-only programs reduce the rate of teen sexual activity.

That's not a particularly surprising conclusion. Last year, Congress' General Accounting Office found that most abstinence-until-marriage programs are

sexual intercourse. In the twenty-first century, many teens choose abstinence for a variety of spiritual, emotional, and physical reasons.

Abstinence for teens usually means postponing sexual activity until they are older, have some life experience, and have found a partner with whom they hope to spend the rest of their life. It means not treating sex casually. It means believing in their own worth and resisting peer pressure to have sex just because everyone else is having it.

not reviewed in a scientifically acceptable manner. Yet Congress has failed to trim the $176 million a year in federal aid that helps support the programs.

Over the past decade, teen pregnancy has been trending downward, as have measures of teen sexual activity. Although abstinence advocates attempt to take credit, health researchers consistently say the actual reason is the fear of contracting sexually transmitted diseases—a risk of which teens are now acutely aware. A newly released federal survey on risky behavior finds that 88% were taught about AIDS and HIV in school. Even so, the same survey found that in 2005, nearly half of all high school students had experienced sexual intercourse. Plainly, banking entirely on abstinence won't work.

What does appear to work is a mix of abstinence training and comprehensive sex education. Multiple studies have found that such programs can both delay first sexual encounters and deter pregnancies and disease. No scientifically rigorous study about abstinence-only programs suggests they can accomplish the same.

Despite those facts, the Bush administration [President George W. Bush] pushed abstinence-only sex education, both in the USA and abroad, with more zeal than scientific realism. Richard Carmona, who served as surgeon general from 2002 to 2006, revealed that the White House insisted for political reasons that he ignore the facts about sex education and focus solely on abstinence.

This is not a time for wishful thinking. New studies suggest the decline in the rate of teens having sex has leveled off.

Texas, where Audelo teaches, is an abstinence-only state. She says most of her students know nothing about herpes. One young woman told Audelo that the HIV virus can be spread through sneezing. They deserve a program that teaches them the risks of sex and guides them toward wise decisions about how to handle it.

—USA TODAY editors

Some teens go as far as to take an abstinence, or virginity, pledge. In the United States, making such a commitment is most common among southern evangelical Christians. The pledge is a promise to God to remain sexually pure until marriage. True Love Waits and the Silver Ring Thing (SRT), the two largest abstinence pledge groups, include millions of members in the United States and worldwide.

Many Christian-based organizations also advocate for an abstinence-only approach to sex education in public schools. Abstinence-only proponents are against more traditional comprehensive sex education, which teaches teens about contraception and how to avoid STDs. Although sex education programs cover abstinence in a positive light, they also give teens information about what to do if they do decide to have sex. Advocates for abstinence-only education, who believe that the Bible forbids sex before marriage, consider such an approach immoral. Decisions about whether schools teach comprehensive sex education (recommended by the medical community) or abstinence-only education are made at the state and local level.

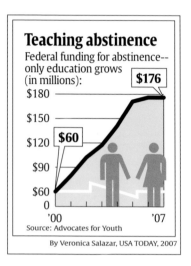

Teaching abstinence

Federal funding for abstinence--only education grows (in millions):

$176

$180

$150

$120 $60

$90

$60

0

'00   '07

Source: Advocates for Youth

By Veronica Salazar, USA TODAY, 2007

SAFER SEX

For teens who do not choose abstinence, there are ways to reduce the risk of catching an STD. The first and foremost involves always using a condom to block the transmission of bacteria and viruses every time a person has sex. Many teens use condoms, although not all make a habit of using one every time they have sex.

Condoms can be purchased in any grocery, drug, or discount store, and no prescription is necessary. Condoms are also commonly available in public restrooms. Many teens, especially males, object to using condoms, claiming that they are too much trouble, are too embarrassing to buy, or are not perfectly reliable. As a matter of fact, it is worth a little trouble and embarrassment to protect oneself

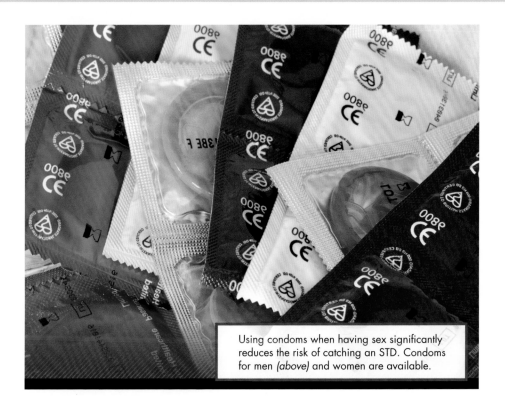

Using condoms when having sex significantly reduces the risk of catching an STD. Condoms for men *(above)* and women are available.

against dangerous STDs such as herpes and HIV/AIDS. And intimate behavior may actually be more enjoyable when partners are not fearful of becoming pregnant or infected with an STD.

If condoms are used correctly, failure rates are only about 2 percent. Many condoms that fail have been stored incorrectly or put on improperly. Although condoms do not offer protection from all sores and lesions or from viral shedding, they do significantly lower the risk of catching an STD. If a person follows instructions for storage and usage that are included in the package, condoms can be up to ten thousand times safer than having unprotected sex.

In 1993 the Food and Drug Administration approved the first female condom, trade named Reality. The device is the first barrier contraceptive for women that provides protection against STDs. It consists of a polyurethane sheath with a flexible ring on each end. The inner ring and sheath are inserted into the vagina. The outer

www.usatoday.com

USA TODAY

News
SECTION A

April 23, 2010

From the Pages of USA TODAY

Women need to take lead in safe sex

In 1993, the Food and Drug Administration gave its stamp of approval to a then-novel item: the female condom. At the time, AIDS awareness was growing. NBA star Magic Johnson had announced he was HIV-positive less than two years earlier. But the virus was still greatly feared and misunderstood. Condom use was urged as a matter of dire public health, and so women finally could protect themselves if their partner chose not to.

Yet according to the Center for Health and Gender Equity, in 2007 about 11 billion male condoms were circulated worldwide compared with 26 million female ones. Cost used to be an issue, but it is no longer: The $4 female condom has been replaced by the 82-cent one.

Though women have, indeed, come a long way, when it comes to sexual equality, we apparently still have a long way to go. But perhaps change is on the way.

I live in Washington, D.C., and if I walk into a participating beauty salon,

ring and a portion of the sheath remain outside the body, partially covering the labia. A number of female condoms are on the market. These are made from a variety of materials, all of which have proven effective in protecting against STDs. Although they are much more affordable than when they first became available, female condoms are still two to three times more expensive than male condoms. Nevertheless, they provide women with the opportunity to protect themselves if their partners choose not to wear a condom.

NAKEESHA AND SERGIO

Nakeesha wants to continue her relationship with Sergio. She finally convenience store or high school, the FC2 female condom (FDA-approved last year) is available free of charge. Washington's campaign to protect women is being promoted through a $500,000 grant from the non-profit MAC AIDS Fund.

Washington has been ravaged by HIV/AIDS, with the highest rate in the country: Over 3% of adults are infected, according to a 2009 epidemiology report. Over a quarter of those are believed to be women. Chicago has launched a female condom awareness campaign, too, and hopefully, other cities will follow. The statistics point to the urgency:

- Women are more vulnerable to contracting sexually transmitted diseases than men, medical research shows. Still, most public funding and marketing efforts have focused only on the male condom.
- A recent National Health and Nutrition Examination Survey estimated that black women have the highest rate of genital herpes (48%) among all groups ages 14 to 49.
- According to the Department of Health and Human Services, AIDS is the leading cause of death among African-American women ages 25–34.
- Black women who live in poverty or have sexual relations with bisexual men are more prone to STDs.

The female condom is only one tool in helping women help themselves, but it's a critical one. It's high time that women have the opportunity to love their men while loving themselves just as much.

—*Yolanda Young*

worked up her courage and talked to him about the behavior that put her and their baby at risk for serious health problems. Sergio told Nakeesha that he had been true to her and that he must have gotten chlamydia before they met. Although she wants to believe him, Nakeesha now asks Sergio to use a condom when they have sex. Nakeesha's first priority is her children, and at least until her baby is born, she has decided to get regular checkups for STDs.

GUIDELINES TO LOWER YOUR RISK

Nakeesha, Sergio, and other teens can take additional steps to reduce the risk of catching or transmitting an STD. These include:

- Limit the number of sexual partners and choose partners carefully.
- Never have any kind of sex or genital contact with someone whose health and sexual practices are unknown to you.
- If a partner's sexual history is unknown, avoiding any activity that puts you in contact with that partner's semen, blood, or other body fluids. This can include deep or open-mouth kissing.
- Talk with a partner about past sexual experiences before having sex. This means knowing that person well enough to be comfortable with talking about intimate matters. Be aware that not everyone is honest about their sexual history.
- Never have sex while under the influence of drugs or alcohol.
- Never share needles or have sex with someone who uses illegal intravenous drugs or who shares needles of any kind.
- Knowing the visible signs and symptoms of STDs. A person should never have sex or be sexually intimate if a partner has signs of infection.
- Use a new condom for each act of sexual intercourse or genital contact.
- Never use natural condoms, called skins, or lambskins. They are more porous than latex condoms and can allow HIV and other viruses to slip through.
- Only use water-based lubricants such as K-Y jelly, Astroglide, Aqua Lube, and glycerin with condoms. Oil-based lubricants such as Vaseline, shortening, mineral oil, massage oil, body lotions, and cooking oil can damage latex condoms.
- Never rely on spermicides containing the ingredient nonoxynol-9 to take the place of a condom. Nonoxynol-9, believed by some to kill STD microbes, is not adequate protection against STDs. It may even increase the risk of

HIV transmission.

- When deciding to have sex, plan ahead to make it as safe as possible. This includes thinking through what to say if an unexpected situation comes up, such as a partner showing signs of an STD.
- Carry a condom if there is the slightest chance of having sex, and use a condom for every sexual encounter. Every teen should be prepared to refuse to have sex if a partner refuses to use a condom.
- Get vaccinated for hepatitis B.
- Go to a doctor or an STD clinic immediately after possible exposure to an STD. Everyone who has multiple sex partners should be checked for STDs by a doctor or health-care provider every six months.

WHO SHOULD BE TESTED FOR STDs?

Teens who are sexually active and meet any of the following criteria should talk to a health-care provider about being tested for STDs:

- Had unprotected sex with a partner and don't know if that person is infected
- Had a new sexual partner within the past sixty days
- Had more than two sexual partners in the past six months
- Had sexual contact with someone with an STD or have been infected with an STD in the past twelve months
- Are pregnant or planning to become pregnant
- Are not consistently using a condom for birth and infection control with new partners
- Have been diagnosed with pelvic inflammatory disease or infections of the urethra, epididymis, or prostate

DARE TO BE EXCEPTIONAL

Avoiding STDs can seem like an extremely complicated process that involves too much discipline and restraint. Even thinking about buying condoms makes many people feel guilty or embarrassed. Trying to decide how to ask a date about his or her sexual history can be mind-boggling to contemplate.

Yet information and help to manage these decisions and choices are available in many places. Teens can talk to someone who is caring, knowledgeable, and nonjudgmental about questions relating to sex, sexual orientation, and sexual relationships. A family member, teacher, counselor, family doctor, or community-based health-care professional could take this role. Teens can learn about STDs from a sex education class in school or from a health provider at an STD clinic. For teens who are nervous about approaching adults, some schools and communities have programs staffed by trained teen volunteers. Books and online resources are other avenues to explore for information.

In order to effectively protect themselves, teens must first acknowledge that anyone can get chlamydia, herpes, or HIV/AIDS if they have sex, especially unprotected sex. They then have to ask themselves—do I want to

USA TODAY Snapshots®

Skewed views on teen sex

About 90% of parents say they talk to their teens about sex, but do they really know what's going on?

High school students who have had sex — 47%

Parents who believe their child is sexually active — 16%

Source: Ipsos-Insight for GlaxoSmithKline and Centers for Disease Control and Prevention

By Julia Neyman and Julie Snider, USA TODAY, 2004

take chances with my health, or am I going to behave responsibly in any sexual relationships I may choose to have now or in the future?

DANIEL AND LEAH

Leah finally decided that her health and well-being were more important than Daniel's desire to have sex. After learning about STDs at the clinic, Leah felt she had a good understanding of the risks she faced. She decided to wait until she was married to have sex. Not surprisingly, her decision made Daniel unhappy. He told Leah that she must think herself better than him and that she could not really love him. Although she is hurt and disappointed by Daniel's reaction, Leah still thinks she made the right decision by protecting her body.

SETTING LIMITS

When it comes to setting sexual boundaries and communicating those boundaries, it's smart to have a discussion with your boyfriend or girlfriend before getting physical. That way, you can minimize the pressure, confusion, and possible arguments and unpleasant scenes that may arise when emotions run high. Here are some guidelines that can make discussions about sex more comfortable and more successful:

- Pick a place to talk where you will not be disturbed or overheard. Don't make it too isolated, however.
- Don't have discussions while under the influence of alcohol or drugs.
- Have an opening line that will ease into the discussion. For instance, begin with "This is a little embarrassing to talk about" or "This is hard to bring up." That gets the awkwardness out in the open and prepares your partner. Then go on with something

like this: "We really seem to like each other, and I think we should talk about how far we're willing to go physically." If you're not sure that the time is right, you can start with, "I have something a little embarrassing to talk about. Is it okay if I bring it up now?" If your partner completely refuses to have such an intimate conversation, then you should make it clear that you are not yet ready to become physically intimate.

- Don't preach or sound judgmental. Talk about your own attitudes and feelings. Begin your sentences with "I think . . ." or "I feel . . ." Encourage your partner to express his or her feelings. Don't press for an instant answer. Your partner might need a few days to sort out his or her feelings.

- Be specific, and try to keep the lines of communication open. Saying, "I don't want to go too far," can lead to misunderstandings. You may have to explain a little more clearly how intimate you are willing to be.

- If you and your partner decide to become sexually active, talk about birth control options as well as ways to minimize the transmission of STDs. Once again, think about lines to ease the awkwardness, such as "I know you're a great person, but I want to be careful. I'd like to talk about birth control and safe sex."

SAY NO TO SEXUAL PRESSURE

Setting boundaries can be hard, and a sexual partner may try to overstep the boundaries you set. He or she may try to force you beyond your boundaries. Rape is the most obvious example of violently forcing someone beyond his or her boundaries. But there are also subtle ways to take advantage of someone sexually. These forms of pressure can be powerful. Verbal pressure is the most common and can be extremely compelling. It can range from put-downs—"You're weird. Nobody waits anymore"—to reassurances—"Don't worry, I've been tested. I'm clean"—to casting doubt on your love—"Is something wrong with me? Don't you love me?"

You can prepare yourself with good answers to any kind of verbal pressure. For example, if some-one is trying to reassure you that he or she is infection free, you can say, "For all you know, I may have an STD. Let's both be safe rather than sorry."

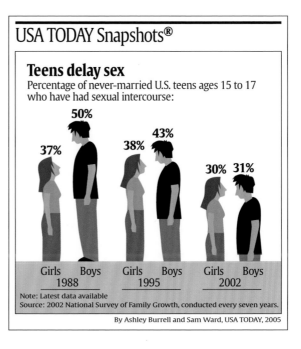

USA TODAY Snapshots®

Teens delay sex
Percentage of never-married U.S. teens ages 15 to 17 who have had sexual intercourse:

50%

43%

37%   38%

30% 31%

Girls Boys   Girls Boys   Girls Boys
  1988   1995   2002

Note: Latest data available
Source: 2002 National Survey of Family Growth, conducted every seven years.

By Ashley Burrell and Sam Ward, USA TODAY, 2005

Often a sexual partner will try to argue you out of your decision. Teens—particularly young women—can feel confident that they don't have to argue with or persuade anyone to accept their beliefs or to think a certain way. Everyone has the right to control his or her own body. It's smart for a teen to say, "No, I don't want to," and stick to it. Friends who really like and respect each other will accept such a stand, even if they don't agree with it. If a partner decides to end the relationship because he or she can't have sex, that decision reveals something about his or her character. It's normal to feel hurt, embarrassed, and rejected in such a situation. But dealing with hurt feelings is much easier than coping with an STD for the rest of your life.

CHAPTER EIGHT

LIVING WITH A CHRONIC STD

T eens can do several things if they discover they are infected with a chronic STD such as herpes, genital warts, or HIV/AIDS. These include being as knowledgeable as possible about STDs, getting necessary treatments, maintaining a healthy lifestyle, and connecting with supportive friends and family for emotional and practical help.

NATHAN

A short time ago, while helping his mother at a church garage sale, Nathan met Janice, another college student. Janice is aware of Nathan's past and accepts that he has HIV. They like each other, but neither knows if they'll have a long-term relationship. Janice helped Nathan connect with a support group, which made him feel less isolated. She also showed him how to use the Internet to tap into the tremendous amount of available information about HIV/AIDs.

BE INFORMED

Teens living with a chronic STD can take control of their health by finding out everything they can about their disease. For instance, if they have genital herpes, they can learn to recognize the prodromal symptoms that may signal an upcoming outbreak. Pinpointing and avoiding foods or situations that trigger outbreaks are also key coping skills. Teens with HIV/AIDS can learn about ways to build up their immune system. They can ask their doctor about new types of treatments and new medications that become available.

Being infected with an STD that causes blisters or sores puts a person at greater risk for catching other STDs. For instance, during a herpes outbreak, a person can more easily contract HIV from an infected partner. Practicing safe sex is vital to ensuring safe and healthy sexual encounters. And keeping sexual partners informed of any health risks is essential.

GET REGULAR MEDICAL CHECKUPS

Regular medical checkups are vital for teens infected with chronic STDs. Prompt detection and diagnosis can lessen the risk of future complications. For instance, young women with genital warts should get regular Pap smears and HPV tests to detect cellular changes that can lead to cervical cancer.

A physician can be an excellent source of information about ways to cope with a chronic STD. When meeting with a doctor, bring a list of your concerns and questions to avoid forgetting or overlooking something while you are in the doctor's office.

Talking with a medical professional about available treatments for STDs, as well as safety information about how to avoid infecting others, is a good way to get essential information.

www.usatoday.com
USA TODAY
Life
SECTION D

October 27, 2008

From the Pages of USA TODAY

Early HIV treatment radically boosts survival

A new analysis of the best time to begin HIV treatment found that starting early sharply improves survival, doctors said Sunday.

Doctors say the new evidence is certain to prompt many doctors to change the way they treat patients, and to prompt health officials to begin examining the evidence underlying guidelines for treating the AIDS virus. The study of 8,374 patients in the USA and Canada showed that those treated later in the course of HIV infection are 70% more likely to die than patients treated sooner, says lead researcher Mari Kitahata of the University of Washington-Seattle.

What makes the finding so striking, Kitahata says, is the "magnitude" of the survival difference between the two study groups.

"Seventy percent is a significant and substantial increase in the risk of death," she says.

The finding surfaced from the biggest comparison of the two treatment strategies ever carried out. The data were drawn from 22 studies conducted from 1996 to 2006 in an attempt to answer a decade-old question about when to begin HIV treatment.

"The guidelines committees are certainly going to look hard at these data next time they meet," says Anthony Fauci, director of the National Institute of Allergy and Infectious Diseases, which sponsored the research.

Current guidelines say that patients should begin treatment only when their levels of a type of white blood cell called CD4 T-cells fall below 350 per cubic millimeter. The AIDS virus targets these cells, which in healthy people throttle up the immune response. But the guidelines have never adequately been tested, Kitahata says.

The new research found that patients fare better when they begin treatment when their CD4 counts are much higher, between 350 and 500 cells per cubic millimeter.

"There's reason to believe you would have even better survival using drugs available now," she says.

Early treatment, however, depends on awareness. Studies show that fewer than four in 10 U.S. adults have been tested for HIV.

—Steve Sternberg

For those teens who cannot afford to go to a doctor, most communities have health departments, infectious disease clinics, STD clinics, women's health clinics, and/or family-planning clinics where testing and treatment are free or low cost and where your personal information is kept confidential. The National STD hotline of the CDC, listed in the Resources section of this book, can help access these types of treatment centers in your specific area.

Drugs that are prescribed to treat an STD should be taken as directed. This may mean taking a pill at a certain time of day or avoiding certain foods while taking certain medications. It is important not to skip doses, combine doses, or stop taking medicine too soon. Doctors, pharmacists, and other health-care providers are always happy to answer patients' questions. Follow-up appointments can ensure that drug side effects are not serious and that prescribed drugs are working as they should.

ADOPT A HEALTHY LIFESTYLE

A strong immune system is a person's best defense against outbreaks of herpes or the progression of HIV/AIDS. Maintaining a healthy lifestyle will help keep the immune system strong. Some factors that make up a healthy lifestyle include:

- Eating right. The United States Department of Agriculture (USDA) Food Guide Pyramid, which places emphasis on grains, fruits, and vegetables and calls for the sparing use of fats, is a sensible guide to follow. The USDA Food Guide Pyramid can be found at http://www.nal.usda.gov/fnic/Fpyr/pmap.htm.
- Getting enough sleep. On average, eight hours of sleep a night is recommended.
- Avoiding the use of cigarettes and the misuse of alcohol and drugs.

- Exercising regularly. The key to making a habit of exercising is to find an activity you enjoy and to stick with it over time.
- Reducing stress through talk therapy, massage, exercise, time with friends and family, and other activities that bring comfort and relaxation.

FIND SOMEONE TO TALK TO

People who learn that they have an STD may feel a range of emotions from fear to depression and shame. Some teens may decide to keep the news a secret from everyone, including their parents and their closest friends. But being open about your health and getting help are key to managing STDs.

Finding someone to talk to about having an STD can make it easier to manage the disease. That person might be a family member, a health-care worker, a counselor, or a support group member (below).

Family and friends are often a source of the strongest support. They can provide valuable guidance and encouragement. Many teens fear and put off telling parents, convinced that they will be judgmental, harsh, and unreasonable. In most cases, parents want to help. The majority will be understanding and willing to do what they can to help their children deal with STDs.

On the other hand, parents and other family members may not be available or supportive. Or they might need additional assistance. In these cases, health-care workers, counselors, trusted adults at school or in some places of worship, hotlines, and online resources are able to provide comfort, insights, and encouragement. Teen volunteers who staff hotlines and community health clinics can be particularly helpful to teens with STDs. A variety of national and local support groups can also help teens. See the Resources section of this book for more information.

REACH OUT TO OTHERS

Teens who accept that they are living with a chronic STD may want to help others learn about prevention and control. There are a variety of ways that teens can become involved, both at school and in the community. For example:

- In health classes, help ensure that the most up-to-date information on STDs is presented. Do some research and give a report on the subject, get permission to create a bulletin board, or line up a special guest speaker.
- Work with school administrators and parents' groups to ensure that students are aware of information that is available about STD prevention. For instance, help counselors send for pamphlets and brochures to give to interested students. Help schedule a speaker who will come to the school and give a presentation at

an assembly. Teens need to be aware that school administrators have to work within state and local sex education guidelines when presenting information on STDs. Some teens may attend an abstinence-only school district, for example. There, education about STD prevention—through any means other than abstinence—will not be permitted.

- Write an editorial or an article for a local newspaper or an online support group about STDs.
- Work with health-care groups in the community. There may be a teen clinic or a teen hotline that needs volunteers and can offer any necessary training.

MIGUEL AND LARISSA

Miguel's doctor advised him to inform all his partners that he has genital warts, but Miguel still couldn't find the courage to tell Larissa. He finally remembered that the clinic he had visited also offered counseling services, so he made another appointment and confided his problem to a nurse there. She was able to give him some suggestions for making the discussion with Larissa a little easier. Miguel knew it would be difficult and that Larissa might leave him. Still, he resolved to do the right thing and tell her about his STD.

HOW DO I TELL MY PARTNER?

Telling a sexual partner—especially a new partner—about a chronic STD infection can be very difficult. Many teens are tempted to avoid doing so. But being open and honest about your sexual health is vital to maintaining good relationships and to protecting your health and your partner's health. Teens can minimize discomfort and embarrassment when breaking the news by thinking through what

Talking to a partner about STDs can be difficult. Try to plan what you are going to say before you start the conversation.

needs to be said and how, when, and where to say it. Some teens decide to role-play with a close friend who they know is accepting. This way, teens can practice what to say and how to respond to a variety of different reactions.

These general guidelines can help make the discussion a little easier:

- If this is just the beginning of a relationship, get to know your partner first. It is not necessary to reveal that you have an STD on the first date, although you must tell your partner before becoming sexually intimate. If you are already in a sexual relationship, you must tell your partner as soon as possible.
- Pick a private place to talk, where you will not be disturbed

or overheard. Pick a neutral place where you are comfortable, preferably not your partner's home. Your home, a park, or the beach are a few possibilities. Talk face-to-face if possible. It's sometimes hard, if not impossible, to pick up nuances or gauge a person's body language in a telephone conversation or text exchange. Some good opening lines could be: "I think I can trust you, so I'd like to tell you something very personal," or "I need to let you know something about me. It may or may not be a big deal to you."

- Have your discussion free of the influence of alcohol or drugs.
- Start your discussion in a nonsexual atmosphere. Don't have your conversation just as you are beginning to have sex or immediately afterward. Instead, choose a time when your thinking is clear.
- Take a calm, matter-of-fact approach. The more positive you are, the more likely it will be that your partner will be calm and positive too. (Try not to use words such as "incurable disease," "terrible problem," or "abnormal.") Be open and honest and answer all questions. Convey to your partner that you know a lot about your STD and how to deal with it to keep you both healthy.
- Give your partner time to adjust. Remember how you felt when you found out you were infected. Don't force a reaction or decision immediately. Avoid becoming angry or judgmental. Treat your partner the way you would like to be treated in the same situation.
- If your partner is accepting of your news, talk about the options— abstinence or safer sex. Be sure to explain how your STD can be spread, so your partner will understand the risks and can take necessary precautions. Encourage your partner to visit a doctor for any testing that might be necessary.

In some cases, news of your STD may be something that your sexual partner can't deal with. That person may choose to walk away from the relationship. If that happens to you, ask for support from your family and friends or from a therapist. Remember that you did the right thing by sharing your news and that you are in charge of your sexual health. On the other hand, many partners will be very understanding and accepting. The way a partner responds to the news of an STD can reveal a great deal about his or her principles, values, and character. If the two of you can find a way to successfully manage sexual health together, you may find the relationship growing stronger.

WHAT IF I WANT TO HAVE CHILDREN?

People who are infected with genital herpes, genital warts, and HIV/AIDS can still have children. They must take steps to ensure that they do not pass their infection on to their children, however. Before becoming pregnant, it is always wise to check with a doctor. Certain medications that are used to control symptoms of STDs can be dangerous for a developing fetus. For this reason, a doctor may suggest changes in treatment if an infected woman is pregnant or nursing a baby.

Proper treatment can dramatically reduce the risk of passing HIV infection from mother to baby during pregnancy. Antiviral medication can prevent an outbreak of herpes that may infect a baby at birth. If a woman is having a herpes outbreak when she is ready to give birth, her doctor may opt to perform a cesarean section to prevent the baby from becoming infected as it passes through the birth canal during a vaginal delivery. In this operation, the doctor delivers the baby through an incision in the mother's abdomen and uterus.

www.usatoday.com

USA TODAY

Life
SECTION D

November 23, 2010

From the Pages of USA TODAY

Gonorrhea at lowest rate since 1941

One of the nation's most common forms of sexually transmitted diseases has fallen to its lowest level ever recorded, but there's still improvement needed, according to a government report out Monday.

The report, part of the Centers for Disease Control and Prevention's annual report card on sexually transmitted diseases (STDs), found that the gonorrhea rate in 2009—the most recent year for which figures are available—was at its lowest level since 1941. The report also found that syphilis rates among women held steady after several years of increases. But the number of U.S. chlamydia cases was up 19% since 2006.

The CDC said that while overall the findings are encouraging, "there are large disparities in STD rates by race and age. Some racial/ethnic minority groups have much higher STD rates than whites, and young African Americans are particularly hard-hit."

Syphilis rates among young black men were about double the rate they were in

UNDERSTANDING THE RISKS

Teens of the twenty-first century live in risky times when it comes to sex and sexual relations. Yet the times look promising, as well. Researchers, doctors, and public health officials are working hard to stem the spread of STDs. In many cases, the numbers of those infected are decreasing. New therapies and drugs to better treat STDs are always becoming available, and the research to find cures is ongoing. Yet, because many STDs are still incurable, the best results can be achieved through prevention. As people continually become

2005, the CDC found. Chlamydia rates reached a record high in 2009, which the CDC said probably represents increased testing for the disease.

Gonorrhea infections in 2009 dropped to about 111 cases per 100,000 population, down 10.5% from 2008. The 2009 rate, the third consecutive annual decline, was the lowest since 1941.

One test can screen for gonorrhea and chlamydia. In 2000, a quarter of women 25 and under were tested for chlamydia, compared with nearly half in 2009.

Once diagnosed, all three reportable STDs are easily treated with antibiotics, said Charlotte Kent, acting director of the CDC's Division of STD Prevention. Although gonorrhea causes symptoms, chlamydia is likely not to, so testing is critical, she said.

"Undiagnosed chlamydia and gonorrhea are preventable causes of infertility," Kent said.

The overall syphilis rate has risen every year since 2001, mostly in men but, more recently, in women. In 2009, there were 4.6 cases per 100,000 population, a 59% jump since 2005.

Jeanne Marrazzo, president of the American Sexually Transmitted Disease Association, called the syphilis rate "alarming."

Rates of all three STDs are higher in blacks than whites, Kent noted. "We've seen some definite signs of progress, but we still see these disparities exist," she said.

The 2009 syphilis rate in blacks was nine times that of whites; in 1999, the difference was 24 times higher.

"It's not an issue of behavior," Kent said, but one related to the fact that the three STDs are more common in blacks.
—*Rita Rubin*

better educated about the risks posed by STDs, they also become more likely to protect themselves.

Teens are also getting the message and are choosing to be more responsible when it comes to sexual relationships. Some have learned the hard way by contracting an STD. Some know friends or family who have had an STD. Some have known people who have died of AIDS. Whatever a person's prior experience, it is never too late to change one's behavior, to protect oneself from STDs, and to get to the doctor and get tested.

GLOSSARY

abstinence: doing without something, for example, alcohol or sexual relations

acquired immunodeficiency syndrome (AIDS): an STD caused by the human immunodeficiency virus (HIV), a retrovirus that destroys the immune system—the body's natural ability to fight disease—and leaves a person open to infection and illness

antibody: a protein produced by the immune system to fight off infection

antigen: a protein, chemical, or bacteria on the surface of an organism that stimulates the production of antibodies

anus: the opening at the lower end of the large intestine through which waste is released

antiretroviral (ARV): a drug used to treat infections caused by retroviruses, such as HIV

autoinoculation: an infection caused by a disease that has spread from another part of the body

carrier: an infected person who may be symptom free but who can pass infection to others

cervix: the neck of the uterus, a narrow passage leading to the vagina

chancre (SHAN-ker): a painless, highly infectious ulcer that is the leading symptom of primary syphilis

chlamydia (kluh-MID-ee-ah): an STD caused by a tiny bacteria, *Chlamydia trachomatis (C. trachomatis)*, chlamydia can infect the urinary-genital area; the anal area; and sometimes the eyes, the throat, and the lungs.

clitoris: the small external female organ of sexual arousal

colposcopy: a procedure by which the vagina is examined using a colposcope, a magnifying and photographic instrument

condom: a close-fitting latex covering worn over the penis during sex to prevent pregnancy and STDs. The female condom is a sheath or a pouch that is inserted into the vagina to prevent pregnancy and STDs.

deoxyribonucleic acid (DNA): a nucleic acid that makes up the genes of all living organisms

dissemination: the process of spreading over or through a large area

ectopic pregnancy: the implantation and development of a fertilized egg outside of the uterus

enzyme-linked immunosorbent assay (ELISA): a diagnostic test in which antigens or antibodies are detected by an enzyme that converts a colorless substance into a colored product

epidemic: an outbreak of disease that spreads more widely or more quickly among a group of people than would normally be expected

epididymis: a tubule, lying on the testicle, through which sperm pass from the testicle to the vas deferens

fallopian tubes: two narrow tubes through which eggs pass from the ovaries to the uterus

fetus: an unborn human offspring after eight weeks of development

genitals: reproductive organs

genital warts: also known as venereal warts. Genital warts are caused by the human papillomavirus (HPV), a family of more than seventy different types of viruses that cause warts on hands, feet, and genitals.

gonorrhea: sometimes called "clap." This is an STD caused by the bacterium *Neisseria gonorrhoeae* (*N. gonorrhoeae*), which produces a number of genital infections and can also infect the mouth, the throat, and the anal area.

hepatitis B: one of a family of hepatitis viruses. Hepatitis B is commonly passed through an exchange of infected body fluids including blood, semen, vaginal secretions, fluid from wounds, and saliva.

herpes: caused by the herpes simplex type 2 virus (HSV-2). This STD is one of a family of viruses that causes cold sores, chicken pox, shingles, and mononucleosis.

highly active antiretroviral therapy (HAART): a powerful combination of antiretroviral drugs (ARVs) prescribed to treat HIV/AIDS

human immunodeficiency virus (HIV): the virus that causes AIDS

human papillomavirus (HPV): a large family of more than seventy different types of viruses that cause warts on hands, feet, and genitals

immune system: a complex body system that aids the body in fighting off disease

immunity: a condition of being protected from disease

infertile: unable to reproduce (for a man, this means unable to make a woman pregnant; for a woman, it means unable to become pregnant)

intravenous: administered into a vein, usually with a needle

labia: fleshy folds that surround the opening of the vagina

lesion: any kind of abnormality of any tissue or organ due to any disease or injury

lymphocytes: a variety of white blood cells consisting of T cells and B cells, both of which are vital to the function of the immune system

monogamous: having a sexual relationship with only one partner during a period of time

neurosyphilis: an infection of the nervous system by *T. pallidum*, the bacterium that causes syphilis

nucleoside analogues: a class of HIV-suppressive drugs that work to keep T cells from making more virus

nucleoside reverse transcriptase inhibitors (NRTIs) and non-nucleoside reverse transcriptase inhibitors (NNRTIs): two classes of HIV-suppressive drugs that block transcription of genetic material inside the virus

opportunistic infections (OIs): conditions caused by microorganisms that may not normally cause disease but that become life threatening when a host's immunity is impaired

ovary: the female reproductive organ that produces eggs and hormones

Pap smear: a test to detect a precancerous or cancerous condition of the cervix

pathogen: an agent such as a bacterium or fungus that causes disease

pelvic inflammatory disease (PID): an infection of the upper female reproductive tract that can lead to infertility

penis: the male reproductive organ that is used to transfer sperm to the female during sexual intercourse

placental barrier: the tissues that protect the fetus by separating its blood from the mother's blood

polymerase chain reaction (PCR): the technique by which a small fragment of genetic material can be rapidly duplicated to produce multiple copies

prodrome: the period of time immediately prior to an outbreak of herpes. Symptoms such as itching, burning, or tingling of the skin can occur during prodrome.

prostate: the male reproductive gland lying below the bladder that produces part of the fluid in semen

protease inhibitors: a class of powerful HIV-suppressive drugs that slow the virus's reproduction process

retrovirus: a family of viruses characterized by a unique mode of replication

ribonucleic acid (RNA): a nucleic acid associated with the control of cellular chemical activity and essential to all forms of life

safe sex: taking precautions to reduce the risk of STD infection or pregnancy when engaging in sexual activity

scrotum: the loose sac of skin and muscles that holds the testicles

semen: a thick white fluid, containing sperm, which is released from the penis during sexual intercourse

seminal vesicle: the male reproductive gland that produces semen

sexually transmitted disease (STD): also known as a sexually transmitted infection (STI), or venereal disease (VD). An STD is a bacterial or viral infection that can be passed from person to person during intimate sexual contact.

shedding: a condition in which the herpes virus is present on the skin and can be easily passed to others. Symptoms of infection may or may not be present.

sperm: male reproductive cells, produced in the testicles

syndrome: the symptomatic phase of a herpes infection

syphilis: an STD caused by the bacterium *Treponema pallidum* (*T. pallidum*). Syphilis can mimic a variety of diseases and can affect virtually every part of the body.

testicle: the male reproductive organ that produces sperm and the hormone testosterone

ulcer: a slow-healing sore

urethra: the tube that carries urine (and in the male, semen) out of the body

uterus: the muscular female reproductive organ in the lower abdomen in which a baby develops before birth

vagina: the muscular tube running from the uterus to the outside of the body; the birth canal

vas deferens: the duct through which sperm is carried from the epididymis to the urethra

vulva: external female sex organs including the clitoris, the vaginal opening, and the labia

Western blot immunoassay test: a diagnostic test that looks for antibodies to infectious agents such as herpes and HIV

yeast infection: an infection by a fungus in the vagina, the mouth, or other parts of the body, causing irritation or other symptoms

RESOURCES

Information about sexually transmitted diseases can be found through a search of the Internet using the key words "Sexually Transmitted Diseases," "STDs," "Sexually Transmitted Infections," "STIs," or the specific name of a disease such as "chlamydia" or "genital herpes." Information can also be obtained by calling or writing the following organizations:

American Academy of Pediatrics (AAP)
141 Northwest Point Boulevard
Elk Grove Village, IL 60007-1098
(847) 434-4000
http://www.aap.org

The AAP's mission is "to attain optimal physical, mental, and social health and well-being for all infants, children, adolescents, and young adults." The organization funds and carries out research and works with the government to ensure that children's health needs are considered when legislation and public policy are developed. Its many publications include manuals on infectious diseases and school health, education brochures, *Healthy Kids* magazine, and a series of child-care books written by AAP members.

American Social Health Association (ASHA)
PO Box 13827
Research Triangle Park, NC 27709
(919) 361-8400
http://www.ashastd.org
http://www.iwannaknow.org

ASHA's aim is to lessen the harmful consequences of STDs on individuals, families, and communities. The organization's website provides information on STDs, support groups, and hotlines. The "I Wanna Know" website is specially designed for teens to learn about STDs and sexual health. ASHA publishes *The Helper*, a newsletter about herpes, and *HPV News*, a publication focusing on human papillomavirus.

CDC National Prevention Information Network (NPIN)
PO Box 6003
Rockville, MD 20849-6003
(800) 458-5231
http://www.cdcnpin.org

NPIN is a national referral, reference, and distribution service sponsored by the CDC. It provides general information about clinics and support groups, answers frequently asked questions, and provides links to other sites. Its education database offers a variety of materials including pamphlets, books, videotapes, posters, and teaching guides.

Centers for Disease Control and Prevention (CDC)
National Center for HIV, STD, and TB Prevention (NCHSTP)
1600 Clifton Road
Atlanta, GA 30333
(800) 232-4636
http://www.cdc.gov/std

The NCHSTP is a leader in preventing the spread of HIV, tuberculosis, and STDs. It carries out research and policy development and assists health departments and other health-care providers to meet community needs. The website provides information on statistics and trends, research, treatment, and links to related sites. Hotlines offer anonymous, confidential information about STDs and how to prevent them. They also provide referrals to clinics and other services.

Free Teens USA
PO Box 97
Westwood, NJ 07675
http://www.freeteensusa.org

Free Teens is an abstinence-centered HIV/AIDS, STDs, and pregnancy prevention program used in many states and countries throughout the world. A variety of publications are available through its website, and the *Free Teens* newsletter is published three times a year.

Hepatitis Foundation International (HFI)
504 Blick Drive
Silver Spring, MD 20904-2901
(800) 891-0707
http://www.hepfi.org

HFI focuses on bringing viral hepatitis under control, supporting research, and educating the public and health-care workers about prevention, diagnosis, and treatment. The foundation has a phone support network, the Patient Advocacy/Information Telecommunication System (PATS).

National Institute of Allergy and Infectious Diseases (NIAID)
Office of Communications and Government Relations
6610 Rockledge Drive
MSC 6612
Bethesda, MD 20892-6612
(301) 496-5717
http://www.niaid.nih.gov

NIAID is part of the National Institutes of Health (NIH), an agency of the U.S. Department of Health and Human Services. NIAID supports biomedical research to prevent, diagnose, and treat illnesses such as AIDS, tuberculosis, and malaria. Its website provides an overview of the immune system, as well as information on vaccine development. Material on experimental treatments can be found under the heading Clinical Trials Database.

Planned Parenthood Federation of America
434 West 33rd Street
New York, NY 10001
(800) 230-PLAN
http://www.plannedparenthood.org

The organization provides information about STDs, as well as referrals to local clinics across the United States.

SELECTED BIBLIOGRAPHY

Goldsmith, Connie. *Hepatitis*. Minneapolis: Twenty-First Century Books, 2011.

Grimes, Jill. *Seductive Delusions: How Everday People Catch STDs*. Baltimore: Johns Hopkins University Press, 2008.

Marr, Lisa. *Sexually Transmitted Diseases: A Physician Tells You What You Need to Know*. Baltimore: Johns Hopkins University Press, 2007.

Schoeberlein, Deborah. *EveryBody: Preventing HIV and Other Sexually Transmitted Diseases among Teens*. Carbondale, CO: RAD Educational Programs, 2001.

Sonenklar, Carol. *AIDS*. Minneapolis: Twenty-First Century Books, 2011.

FURTHER READING AND WEBSITES

Books

Brequet, Amy. *Chlamydia.* The Library of Sexual Health series. New York: Rosen Publishing Group, 2006.

Ford, Carol A. *Living with Sexually Transmitted Diseases.* Teen's Guides. New York: Facts on File, 2009.

Freedman, Jeri. *Hepatitis B.* The Library of Sexual Health series. New York: Rosen Publishing Group, 2009.

Goldsmith, Connie. *Invisible Invaders: Dangerous Infectious Diseases.* Minneapolis: Twenty-First Century Books, 2006.

Johns Hopkins AIDS Institute. *The Guide to Living with HIV.* Baltimore: Johns Hopkins University Press, 2006.

Michaud, Christopher. *Gonorrhea.* The Library of Sexual Health. New York: Rosen Publishing Group, 2006.

Murray, Patrick R., Ken S. Rosenthal, and Michael A. Pfaller. *Medical Microbiology.* 5th ed. Philadelphia: Elsevier, 2005.

Silverstein, Alvin, Virginia B. Silverstein, and Laura Silverstein Nunn. *The STDs Update.* Springfield, NJ: Enslow Publishers, 2010.

Websites

The Mayo Clinic
http://www.mayoclinic.com/health/sexually-transmitted-diseases-stds/DS01123

The nonprofit Mayo Clinic is one of the best-respected medical institutions in the United States. The Mayo Clinic's website provides authoritative, accessible information on the most common STDs.

Medline Plus
http://www.medlineplus.gov

An online resource provided by the National Library of Medicine and the National Institutes of Health, Medline Plus has extensive, easily searchable information on STDs.

National Institutes of Health
http://health.nih.gov/topic/SexuallyTransmittedDiseases

A goal of the NIH is to improve the health of Americans through understanding the "causes, diagnosis, prevention, and cure of human diseases." The sexually transmitted diseases section of the NIH websites provides the public with a depth of well-researched information on STDs and other sexual health topics.

Teen Health & Wellness: Real Life, Real Answers
http://www.teenhealthandwellness.com/

This online resource provides an extensive database of "nonjudgmental, straightforward" articles on topics of concern to teens, including drugs, diseases, and alcohol.

TeensHealth
http://kidshealth.org/teen/sexual_health/

TeensHealth offers teens easy-to-follow, doctor-approved information. The website is funded by the Nemours Foundation, a nonprofit organization dedicated to issues of children's health.

LERNER

SOURCE

Expand learning beyond the printed book. Download free, complementary educational resources for this book from our website, www.lerneresource.com

INDEX

ABOUT THE AUTHOR

Diane Yancey is the author of more than thirty-five books for middle-grade and high school readers. She has written on topics that range from the Civil War to serial killers. She and her husband live in the Pacific Northwest with three cats, Newton, Lily, and Alice.

PHOTO ACKNOWLEDGMENTS

The images in this book are used with the permission of: © Ed White/Taxi/Getty Images, pp. 1, 3; © Monkey Business Images/Dreamstime.com, p. 10; © Marcus Halevi/USA TODAY, p. 13; © Adrian Weinbrecht/Iconica/Getty Images, p. 18; © Laura Westlund/Independent Picture Service, pp. 21, 23, 58-59; © David Phillips/Visuals Unlimited, Inc., p. 27; © Phillippe Garo/Photo Researchers, Inc., p. 32; © Jym Wilson/ USA TODAY, p. 55; © Eileen Blass/USA TODAY, p. 85; © Martin M. Rotker/Photo Researchers, Inc., p. 86; © Peter Dazeley/Photographer's Choice/Getty Images, p. 88; © Adam Hart-Davis/SPL/Photo Researchers, Inc., p. 95; © iStockphoto.com/ AlexRaths, p. 105; © Jose L. Pelaez/Comet/CORBIS, p. 108; © Kristy-Anne Glubish/ Design Pics Inc./Alamy, p. 111.

Front cover: © Ed White/Taxi/Getty Images.

Main body text set in USA TODAY Roman 10/15